Learn English with Cartoons

A Fun Vocabulary Builder Workbook

Contents

INTRODUCTION

Learning a new language can be a terrifying and unbelievable task. However, it may seem that only children can learn a new language and by the time you are an adult, it is simply too late. That is not the case. Adults everyday learn new things in their careers and in their daily activities. Learning a new language is no different. Spending a few minutes each day learning one part of the language is the best way to approach this beneficial skill. Being bilingual is an ability that will provide you with more employment opportunities in your career. Needless to say, right now would be a great time to gain one of the most important talents to be successful – learning English.

To learn English, vocabulary is one of the key parts. Learning specific vocabulary words grouped by themes allows you to be able to identify everyday objects. Once this is done, sentences can be put together in order to increase your conversational skills. Putting these vocabulary words into the sentences and then learning the order of the words in the sentence increases your knowledge of reading, writing, listening and speaking English. Communicating in English allows you to build upon your prior knowledge of the vocabulary and parts of speech learned in order to move onto the structures of the sentences. Before you know it, you will be communicating in English with your friends and family.

In this book, you will learn about daily activities as well as common topic conversations. The book is set up so that it begins with the initial skills and vocabulary needed to learn before moving to more difficult and challenging grammar skills and vocabulary situations. The book also begins with the themes that apply specifically to you and then move to activities and ideas that you would experience with other people or throughout your life.

Each chapter is divided into vocabulary with a pronunciation key to help you learn how to accurately pronounce each vocabulary word that may be new to you. Focusing on this section of each chapter first will allow you to practice saying the words correctly before moving on to the grammatical and writing skills. Each vocabulary word is in a simple sentence so you can understand in what context you would be exposed to this word.

The next section of the chapter is set aside for the grammatical skills that apply to both the theme of the chapter and the writing and reading skills. An explanation is included for that grammar skill as well as many examples and explanations. Once you acquire the information about the grammar skill, you can move to the next section about reading a situation presented in a cartoon or comic format using the vocabulary words for that chapter. Each comic includes both sentences, common expressions and phrases as well as detailed pictures for you to understand what is taking place in that reading section.

Lastly, the chapter contains activities that include the vocabulary in addition to the grammar, reading and writing skills that you learned in that chapter. Each activity is presented in a fun and interesting way, but these activities also were created in a way so that you would use them in your daily life. For example, some of the activities include composing a text message based on the thematic situation or responding to an email.

What sets this book apart from the other language learning books out on the market is that this book includes tips, images and explanations so that you thoroughly learn each part needed before moving onto the more challenging skills. Additionally, the activities are presented using real-world situations that you would experience in the workplace and so that you could quickly hold a conversation or read material in English.

MAKING THE MOST OF THIS BOOK

To make sure that you get the most of this book, there are 20 chapters dedicated to a specific theme and grammar skill. For every 5 chapters, there is a thorough review of the vocabulary, reading, grammar and writing skills that will allow you to incorporate what you learned with the vocabulary and grammar. You will be able to bring these skills together to create sentences whether you are writing or speaking. After the review, there is a test covering the skills from the review and information in the chapter. Completing this test will show you your progress.

To better develop your English skills, it is necessary for you to apply what you learn from this book as you learn to your own life. This means that you need to speak, read and write English during your day. Take the vocabulary words that you use and see if you can identify them as you go about your day. Possibly, speak to a friend who wants to learn English too. You may also want to begin reading the news or other informative information in English.

SUGGESTIONS FOR LEARNING ENGLISH

It is easy to complete this book and then go back to speaking your native language. Learning English is a never-ending process. Consider these suggestions in order to continue your journey of learning English.

- Find friends who speak English and talk to them, even if you are only speaking a few words.
- Read novels that interest you, even if you have already read them in your native language.
- Use both signs that you see in English to connect a picture to an English word.
- Write in English and then check to make sure you are writing it correctly.

These are just a few suggestions about using what you have learned in this book in order to be successful in being a fluent English speaker.

Chapter 1: Who am I?

KEY VOCABULARY WORDS AND SENTENCES

age [āj]
Sentence: My age is 10.

boy [boi]
Sentence: Tom is a boy.

down [doun] or [dăwn]
Sentence: Write down your name.

five [fīv]
Sentence: I am five years old.

girl [gƏrl]
Sentence: The girl is Sally.

Hi [hī]
Sentence: Hi!

how [hou] or [hăw]
Sentence: How are you?

meet [mēt]
Sentence: It is nice to meet you.

my [mī]
Sentence: My name is Tom.

name [nām]
Sentence: Her name is Sally.

new [noo]
Sentence: I am new here.

nice [nīs]
Sentence: You are nice.

old [ohld]
Sentence: I am 10 years old.

Pat [păt]
Sentence: Her name is Pat.

road [rōd]
Sentence: I walk on the road.

Sally [săl – ē]
Sentence: Sally is a girl.

school [skool]
Sentence: I go to school.

seven [sĕv – ĭn]
Sentence: I am seven years old.

student [stoo – dĭnt]
Sentence: I am a student.

Tom [tŏm]
Sentence: I am Tom.

town [toun] or [tăwn]
Sentence: I live in town.

welcome [wĕl – kŭhm]
Sentence: Welcome!

what [whŭt]
Sentence: What is your name?

where [wār]
Sentence: Where do you live?

years [yērs]
Sentence: I am 6 years old.

your [yor]
Sentence: Your name is Sally.

GRAMMAR

Look at the chart below.
Use the verb next to the pronoun or noun in the chart to make sentences.

PRONOUN OR NOUN	VERB
I	Am
She	Is
He	Is
You	Are
We	Are
They	Are
It	Is
(names) - Sally, Sam, Tom, Pat	Is

Create sentences in this way.

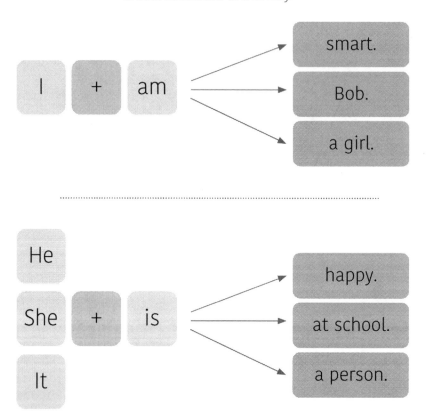

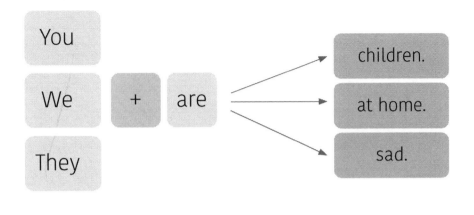

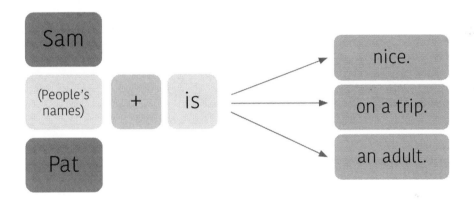

Read the examples below.

1. **I** <u>am</u> a student.
2. **She** <u>is</u> a student.
3. **He** <u>is</u> a student.
4. **You** <u>are</u> a student.
5. **We** <u>are</u> students.
6. **They** <u>are</u> students.
7. **It** <u>is</u> a student.
8. **Sam** <u>is</u> a student.
9. **Pat** <u>is</u> a student.

PRACTICE

Part 1 Directions: Read each part of the conversation. Fill in the bubbles or blanks. What should you say?

Part 2 Directions: Fill in the introduction graphic organizer.

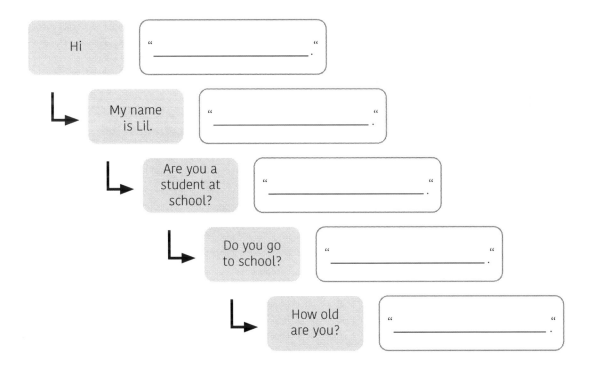

Chapter 2: ASKING FOR DIRECTIONS AND INFORMATION

KEY VOCABULARY WORDS AND SENTENCES

again [Ə - gĭn}
Sentence: I will do that again.

better [bēt – tƏr]
Sentence: Apples taste better than oranges.

close [clōz]
Sentence: Close the door!

does [dŭz]
Sentence: She does not like you.

drugstore [drŭg - stór]
Sentence: They drove to the drugstore.

easy [ē – zē]
Sentence: The test is easy.

first [fƏrst]
Sentence: Turn at the first street.

go [gō]
Sentence: Go straight.

hurry [hƏr – rē]
Sentence: Hurry up!

left [lĕft]
Sentence: Turn left at the light.

next [nĕxt]
Sentence: Turn onto the next street.

oak [ōk]
Sentence: That is an oak tree.

pine [pīn]
Sentence: I live on Pine Street.

right [rīt]
Sentence: I write with my right hand.

second [sĕc – ŭnd]
Sentence: Take a second right.

soon [sün]
Sentence: We will get there soon.

straight [strāt]
Sentence: The house is straight ahead.

street [strēt]
Sentence: We live on this street.

take [tāk]
Sentence: Take the next left.

third [thƏrd]
Sentence: Our house is the third one on the right.

turn [tƏrn]
Sentence: Turn onto this street.

where [wār]
Sentence: Where is your house?

what [wŭt]
Sentence: What is your name?

who [hü]
Sentence: Who are you?

which [wĭch]
Sentence: Which street should I take?

GRAMMAR

Questions may begin with **WHO, WHERE, WHEN, WHAT** or **WHICH**.
The answer to a **WHO** question will be a <u>person</u>.
The answer to a **WHERE** question will be a <u>place</u>.
The answer to a **WHEN** question will be a <u>time</u>.
The answer to a **WHAT** question will be a <u>thing</u>.
The answer to a **WHICH** question will be a <u>choice between two</u> things.

QUESTIONS SHOULD START WITH

ANSWERS SHOULD BE

QUESTION	ANSWER	
WHO	A PERSON	
WHERE	A PLACE	
WHEN	A TIME	
WHAT	A THING	
WHICH	PICK	

Read the questions and answers below.

Who are you?

Tim

I am Tim.

Who is at the door?

Rob

Rob is at the door.

Where do you live?

I live in a house.

Where are you going?

I am going to the park.

When is the party?

The party is at 8:00 p.m.

When do you leave work?

I leave work at 10:10 a.m.

What is on the shelf?

Books are on the shelf.

What is your age?

My age is seventy.

Which one do you like to eat?

I want pizza.

Which way do we go?

I will go to the right.

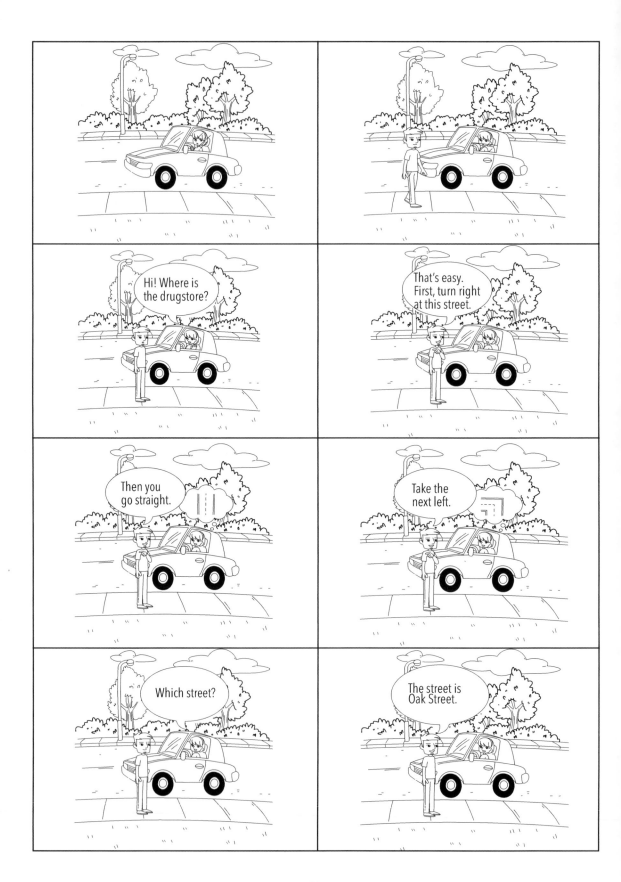

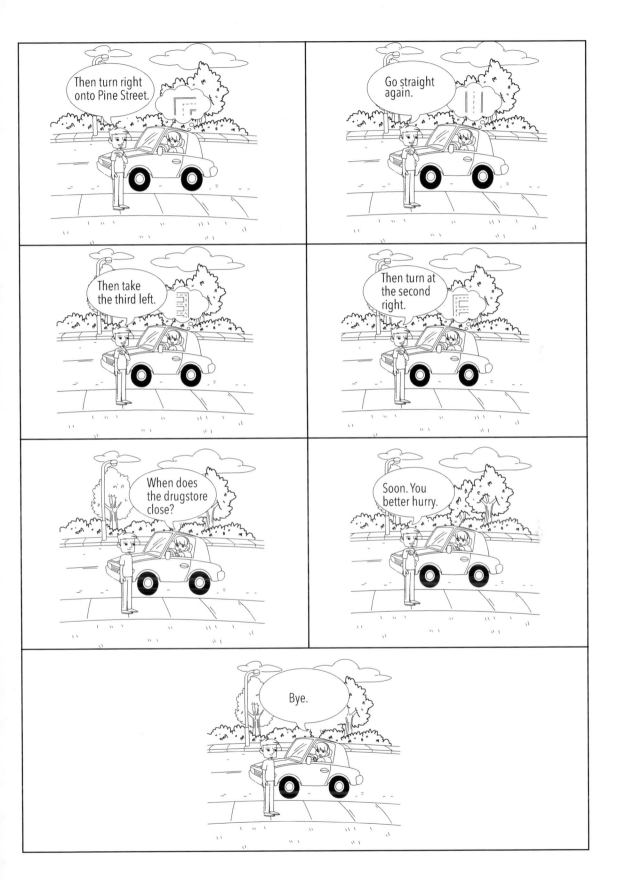

PRACTICE

Part 1 Directions: Look at the picture. Read each answer. Write the question that matches each answer. Remember the question starters–WHO, WHERE, WHEN, WHAT, and WHICH.

Question: _____ is the woman?

Answer: The woman is at the drugstore.

Question: _____ is the person?

Answer: She is a woman.

Question: _____ did the woman go to the drugstore?

Answer: She went to the drugstore at 2:00 p.m.

Question: _____ did the woman get at the drugstore?

Answer: She got medicine.

Question: _____ drug did the woman get?

Answer: She got this one.

Part 2 Directions: Look at the map. Help the man give directions to the woman.

"First, go straight on Main _____. _____, turn _____ on Pine Street. Then, turn _____ on _____ Street. Next, _____ right on River _____. Go _____ on River Street. Then, _____ _____ on Hill Street. Last, turn left on _____ Street. You are now at the school!"

Where is the school? How do I get there?

MAIN STREET

PINE STREET

MAPLE STREET

RIVER STREET

HILL STREET

GROVE STREET

SCHOOL

Chapter 3: FAMILY AND RELATIONSHIPS

KEY VOCABULARY WORDS AND SENTENCES

ate [āt]
Sentence: I ate pizza.

aunt [ant]
Sentence: My mom's sister is my aunt.

brother [brŭ – thƏr]
Sentence: I love my brother.

cake [cāk]
Sentence: Cake tastes great.

cousin [cŭz - ĭn]
Sentence: My cousin lives close by.

family [fam – ĭ – lē]
Sentence: I live with my family.

father [fŏ - th Ər]
Sentence: My father and brother play ball.

Fred [frĕd]
Sentence: Fred is my brother.

grandfather [grand – fŏ - th Ər]
Sentence: My grandfather is old.

grandmother [grand – mŭ – thƏr]
Sentence: My grandmother likes to bake.

mother [mŭ – thƏr]
Sentence: My mother is a nurse.

Sally [săl – ē]
Sentence: Sally is a student.

sister [sĭs – tƏr]
Sentence: I live with my sister.

son [sŭn]
Sentence: My mother has a son.

uncle [ŭn cƏl]
Sentence: My mother's brother is my uncle.

GRAMMAR

PRONOUNS:

GIRL OR WOMAN	BOY OR MAN	ONE THING	MYSELF
SHE	HE	IT	I
HER	HIM		ME

Subject pronouns are usually placed before the verb.
Most of the time, they are near the beginning of the sentence.

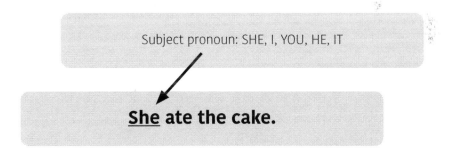

Subject pronoun: SHE, I, YOU, HE, IT

<u>She</u> ate the cake.

Object pronouns are usually after the verb.
They come near the end of the sentence.

Object pronoun: HER, ME, YOU, IT, HIM

The dog likes <u>him</u>.

Who ate the cake? A family picture of them.

PRACTICE

Part 1 Directions: Look at the family tree. Complete the crossword puzzle by writing how each pair of family members are related.

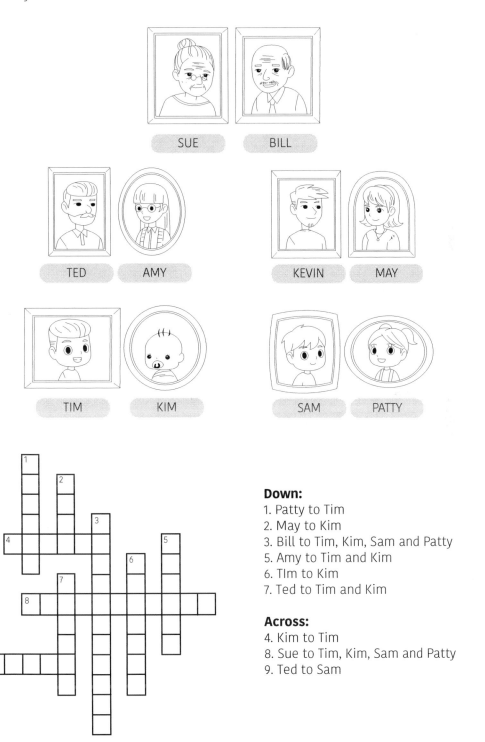

SUE   BILL

TED   AMY   KEVIN   MAY

TIM   KIM   SAM   PATTY

Down:
1. Patty to Tim
2. May to Kim
3. Bill to Tim, Kim, Sam and Patty
5. Amy to Tim and Kim
6. TIm to Kim
7. Ted to Tim and Kim

Across:
4. Kim to Tim
8. Sue to Tim, Kim, Sam and Patty
9. Ted to Sam

Part 2 Directions: Read each text message. Then fill in the blank with the correct family member.

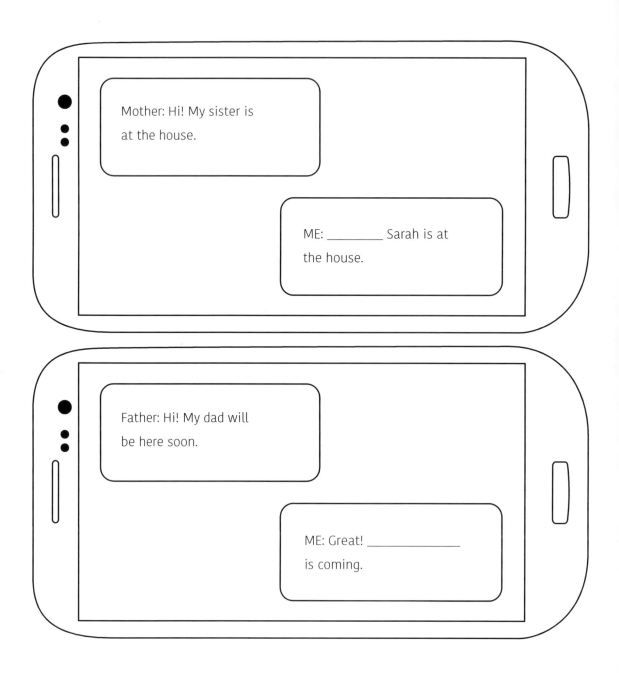

Mother: Hi! My sister is
at the house.

ME: _____ Sarah is at
the house.

Father: Hi! My dad will
be here soon.

ME: Great! _____
is coming.

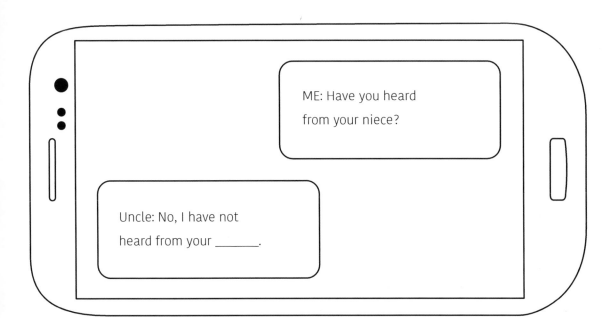

ME: Have you heard from your niece?

Uncle: No, I have not heard from your _____.

Chapter 4: HOUSES

KEY VOCABULARY WORDS AND SENTENCES

bathroom [băth – rūm]
Sentence: The bathroom is next to the bedroom.

bedroom [bĕd – rūm]
Sentence: A bed is in my bedroom.

Billy [bĭl – ē]
Sentence: Billy is my brother.

child [chīld]
Sentence: The child is young.

children [chĭl – drĭn]
Sentence: My mother has two children.

closet {clŏ – zĕt]
Sentence: A closet is in the bedroom.

drawer [drȯ - Ər]
Sentence: I put clothes in the drawers.

hall [hŏl]
Sentence: We walk down the hall.

kitchen [kĭch – ĭn]
Sentence: Food is in the kitchen.

living room [lĭv – ing rūm]
Sentence: My family is in the living room.

man [man]
Sentence: There is one man in the room.

men [mĭn]
Sentence: There are two men in the room.

mice [mīs]
Sentence: The three mice are in the cage.

mouse [maus]
Sentence: The mouse ate cheese.

tables [tā – bƏl]
Sentence: There are three tables in the house.

teeth [tēth]
Sentence: I brush my teeth.

tooth [tüth]
Sentence: My tooth hurts.

toy [tȯi]
Sentence: I played with my toy.

two [tū]
Sentence: I have two sisters.

under [ŭn – dƏr]
Sentence: The book is under the bed.

woman [wu̇ – mƏn]
Sentence: One woman walks on the street.

women [wĭ – mĭn]
Sentence: Two women are in the room.

GRAMMAR

Read about singular and plural nouns.

> **NOUNS** – person, place or thing
> **SINGULAR** – one
> **PLURAL** – two or more

SINGULAR NOUNS   **PLURAL NOUNS**

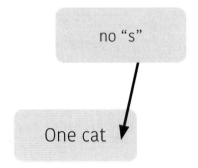 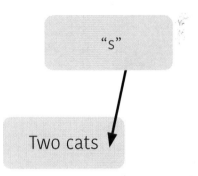

SINGULAR	**PLURAL**
• child	• children
• man	• men
• mouse	• mice
• tooth	• teeth
• woman	• women

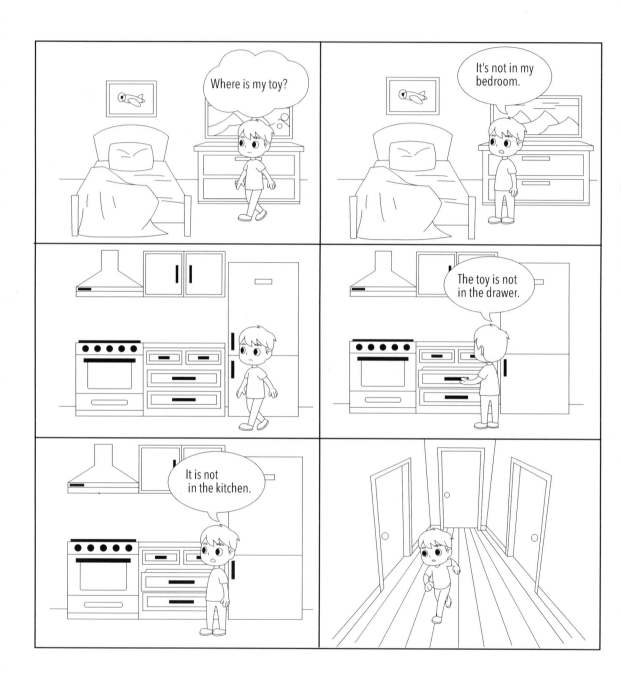

PRACTICE

Part 1 Directions: Write the rooms from the directions. Draw the things in each room.

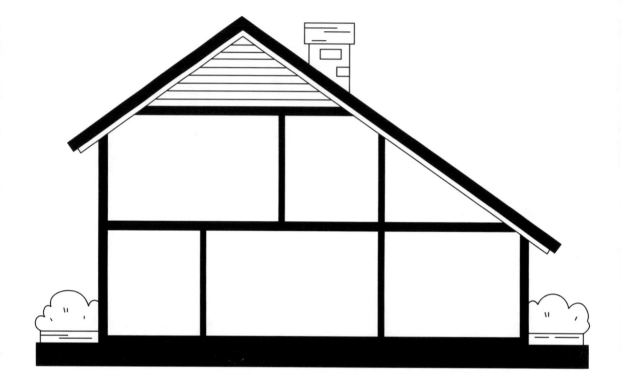

Write the correct room in the right place.

1. The room on the right on the first floor is the KITCHEN.
2. The room to the left of the kitchen is the LIVING ROOM.
3. The room on the second floor on the left is the BEDROOM.
4. The room to the right of the bedroom is the BATHROOM.
5. The room to the right of the bathroom is the HALL.

Draw the things in the right rooms.

1. Draw two beds in the bedroom.
2. Draw three tables in the house. One table is in the kitchen, one table is in the bathroom, and one table is in the living room.
3. Draw one closet in the bedroom.
4. Draw five toys in the living room.

PRACTICE

Part 2 Directions: Read the riddle. Write down the room that the riddle describes.

1. I eat food here.

I cook in here.

_____

2. I sit and watch TV in here.

My family talks in here.

_____

3. There is water is in this room.

I brush my teeth in here, too.

_____

4. I walk in this room.

Not much happens here.

_____

Chapter 5: SCHOOL AND WORK

KEY VOCABULARY WORDS AND SENTENCES

after [ăf - tǝr]
Sentence: Monday is after Sunday.

April [ā – prĭl]
Sentence: Flowers bloom in April.

August [ŏ – gŭst]
Sentence: Summer ends in August.

before [bē – for]
Sentence: A comes before B.

December [dē – sĭm – bǝr]
Sentence: Snow falls in December.

everyone [ĕv – rē – wŭn]
Sentence: Everyone loves summer.

February [fĕb – ū -wār – rē]
Sentence: It is still cold in February.

Friday [frī – dā]
Sentence: I love Friday.

January [jan – ū– wār – rē]
Sentence: January is the first month.

July [jū – lī]
Sentence: July is a hot month.

June [jūn]
Sentence: Summer begins in June.

late [lāt]
Sentence: I don't want to be late for school.

March [märch]
Sentence: February comes before March.

May [mā]
Sentence: It rains in May.

Monday [mŭn – dā]
Sentence: School starts on Monday.

month [mŭnth]
Sentence: There are twelve months in the year.

November [nō – vĭm – bǝr]
Sentence: November comes after October.

o'clock [ō – clŏk]
Sentence: It is twelve o'clock.

October [ŏc – tō – bǝr]
Sentence: October comes after September.

Saturday [săt – ǝr – dā]
Sentence: I will play on Saturday.

September [sĕp – tĭm – bǝr]
Sentence: My birthday is in September.

seven [sĕv – ĭn]
Sentence: There are seven days in a week.

six [sĭks]
Sentence: There are six people in my family.

Sunday [sŭn – dā]
Sentence: Sunday comes after Saturday.

thirty [thǝr – tē]
Sentence: Four months have thirty days.

Thursday [thǝrz – dā]
Sentence: Thursday comes before Friday.

today [tǝ – dā]
Sentence: Today is Wednesday.

Tuesday [tūz – dā]
Sentence: Tuesday comes after Monday.

Wednesday [wĭnz – dā]
Sentence: Wednesday comes before Thursday.

work [wǝrk]
Sentence: I go to work during the week.

GRAMMAR

Look at the months of the year.

JANUARY

S	M	T	W	T	F	S
					1	2
3	4	5	6	7	8	9
10	11	12	13	14	15	16
17	18	19	20	21	22	23
24	25	26	27	28	29	30
31						

FEBRUARY

S	M	T	W	T	F	S
	1	2	3	4	5	6
7	8	9	10	11	12	13
14	15	16	17	18	19	20
21	22	23	24	25	26	27
28						

MARCH

S	M	T	W	T	F	S
	1	2	3	4	5	6
7	8	9	10	11	12	13
14	15	16	17	18	19	20
21	22	23	24	25	26	27
28	29	30	31			

APRIL

S	M	T	W	T	F	S
				1	2	3
4	5	6	7	8	9	10
11	12	13	14	15	16	17
18	19	20	21	22	23	24
25	26	27	28	29	30	

MAY

S	M	T	W	T	F	S
						1
2	3	4	5	6	7	8
9	10	11	12	13	14	15
16	17	18	19	20	21	22
23	24	25	26	27	28	29
30	31					

JUNE

S	M	T	W	T	F	S
		1	2	3	4	5
6	7	8	9	10	11	12
13	14	15	16	17	18	19
20	21	22	23	24	25	26
27	28	29	30			

JULY

S	M	T	W	T	F	S
				1	2	3
4	5	6	7	8	9	10
11	12	13	14	15	16	17
18	19	20	21	22	23	24
25	26	27	28	29	30	31

AUGUST

S	M	T	W	T	F	S
1	2	3	4	5	6	7
8	9	10	11	12	13	14
15	16	17	18	19	20	21
22	23	24	25	26	27	28
29	30	31				

SEPTEMBER

S	M	T	W	T	F	S
			1	2	3	4
5	6	7	8	9	10	11
12	13	14	15	16	17	18
19	20	21	22	23	24	25
26	27	28	29	30		

OCTOBER

S	M	T	W	T	F	S
					1	2
3	4	5	6	7	8	9
10	11	12	13	14	15	16
17	18	19	20	21	22	23
24	25	26	27	28	29	30
31						

NOVEMBER

S	M	T	W	T	F	S
	1	2	3	4	5	6
7	8	9	10	11	12	13
14	15	16	17	18	19	20
21	22	23	24	25	26	27
28	29	30				

DECEMBER

S	M	T	W	T	F	S
			1	2	3	4
5	6	7	8	9	10	11
12	13	14	15	16	17	18
19	20	21	22	23	24	25
26	27	28	29	30	31	

January comes <u>before</u> February.	April comes <u>after</u> March.

JANUARY

S	M	T	W	T	F	S
					1	2
3	4	5	6	7	8	9
10	11	12	13	14	15	16
17	18	19	20	21	22	23
24	25	26	27	28	29	30
31						

FEBRUARY

S	M	T	W	T	F	S
	1	2	3	4	5	6
7	8	9	10	11	12	13
14	15	16	17	18	19	20
21	22	23	24	25	26	27
28						

MARCH

S	M	T	W	T	F	S
	1	2	3	4	5	6
7	8	9	10	11	12	13
14	15	16	17	18	19	20
21	22	23	24	25	26	27
28	29	30	31			

APRIL

S	M	T	W	T	F	S
				1	2	3
4	5	6	7	8	9	10
11	12	13	14	15	16	17
18	19	20	21	22	23	24
25	26	27	28	29	30	

MAY

S	M	T	W	T	F	S
						1
2	3	4	5	6	7	8
9	10	11	12	13	14	15
16	17	18	19	20	21	22
23	24	25	26	27	28	29
30	31					

JUNE

S	M	T	W	T	F	S
		1	2	3	4	5
6	7	8	9	10	11	12
13	14	15	16	17	18	19
20	21	22	23	24	25	26
27	28	29	30			

JULY

S	M	T	W	T	F	S
				1	2	3
4	5	6	7	8	9	10
11	12	13	14	15	16	17
18	19	20	21	22	23	24
25	26	27	28	29	30	31

AUGUST

S	M	T	W	T	F	S
1	2	3	4	5	6	7
8	9	10	11	12	13	14
15	16	17	18	19	20	21
22	23	24	25	26	27	28
29	30	31				

SEPTEMBER

S	M	T	W	T	F	S
		1	2	3	4	
5	6	7	8	9	10	11
12	13	14	15	16	17	18
19	20	21	22	23	24	25
26	27	28	29	30		

OCTOBER

S	M	T	W	T	F	S
					1	2
3	4	5	6	7	8	9
10	11	12	13	14	15	16
17	18	19	20	21	22	23
24	25	26	27	28	29	30
31						

NOVEMBER

S	M	T	W	T	F	S
	1	2	3	4	5	6
7	8	9	10	11	12	13
14	15	16	17	18	19	20
21	22	23	24	25	26	27
28	29	30				

DECEMBER

S	M	T	W	T	F	S
			1	2	3	4
5	6	7	8	9	10	11
12	13	14	15	16	17	18
19	20	21	22	23	24	25
26	27	28	29	30	31	

Look at the days of the week.

Sunday	Monday	Tuesday	Wednesday	Thursday	Friday	Saturday
		1	2	3	4	5
6	7	8	9	10	11	12
13	14	15	16	17	18	19
20	21	22	23	24	25	26
27	28	29	30	31		

Monday comes <u>before</u> Tuesday.

Saturday comes <u>after</u> Friday.

Sunday	Monday	Tuesday	Wednesday	Thursday	Friday	Saturday
		1	2	3	4	5
6	7	8	9	10	11	12
13	14	15	16	17	18	19
20	21	22	23	24	25	26
27	28	29	30	31		

PRACTICE

Part 1 Directions: Match the months and days to their descriptions.

_____1. February   A. month after February

_____2. August   B. month before May

_____3. May   C. month after August

_____4. September   D. month before February

_____5. December   E. month after July

_____6. June   F. month before November

_____7. November   G. month after April

_____8. January   H. month before December

_____9. April   I. month after November

_____10. October   J. month before March

_____11. July   K. month after June

_____12. March   L. month before July

....

_____13. Wednesday   A. day after Wednesday

_____14. Saturday   B. day after Saturday

_____15. Monday   C. day before Tuesday

_____16. Thursday   D. day after Thursday

_____17. Sunday   E. day before Sunday

_____18. Tuesday   F. day after Monday

_____19. Friday   G. day before Thursday

PRACTICE

Part 2 Directions: Read each clue. Which day or month is being described from the clues?

1. Clue 1: The day is not Saturday.

   Clue 2: The day is Tuesday, Wednesday, or Sunday.

   Clue 3: The day is not a school day.

   The day is _____.

2. Clue 1: The month is after March and before October.

   Clue 2: The month is not April or July.

   Clue 3: The month has thirty-one days in it.

   Clue 4: The month does not begin with "A."

   The month is _____.

3. Clue 1: The day is a school day.

   Clue 2: The day is after Sunday.

   Clue 3: The day begins with a "T."

   Clue 4: The day is before Wednesday.

   The day is _____.

4. Clue 1: The month is near the beginning of the year.

   Clue 2: The month is not February.

   Clue 3: The month begins with "J."

   The month is _____.

5. Clue 1: The month is in the summer.

   Clue 2: The month's name has four letters in it.

   Clue 3: The month ends in "y."

   The month is _____.

Review and Advancement for Chapters 1 through 5

Chapter 1 Directions: Fill in the blanks.

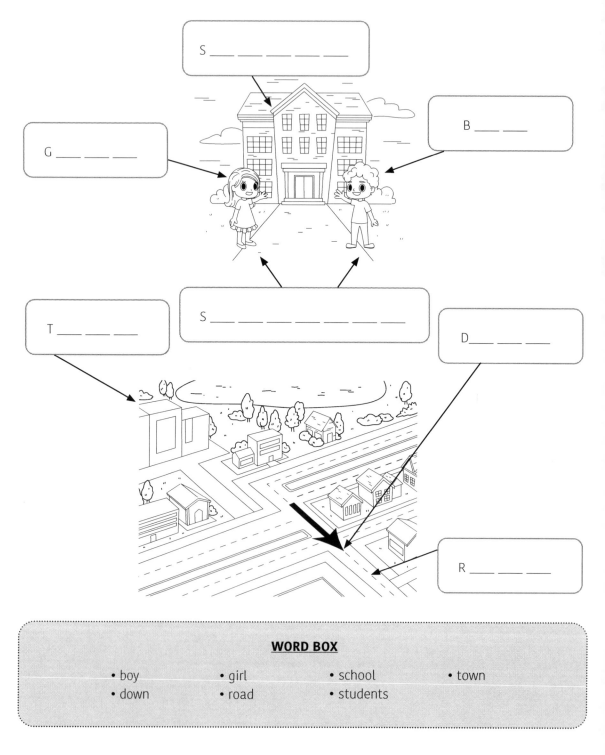

S __ __ __ __ __ __

B __ __ __

G __ __ __ __

T __ __ __ __

S __ __ __ __ __ __ __ __

D__ __ __ __

R __ __ __ __ __

WORD BOX

- boy
- girl
- school
- town
- down
- road
- students

S __ __ __ __

Y __ __ __ __ __ O __ __ __

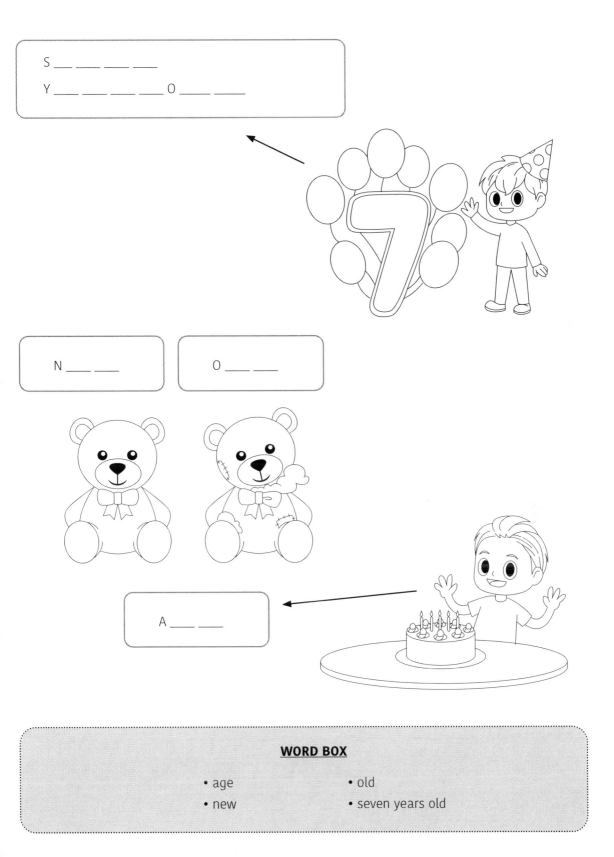

N __ __

O __ __

A __ __ __

WORD BOX

- age
- old
- new
- seven years old

Chapter 2 Directions: Fill in the blanks.

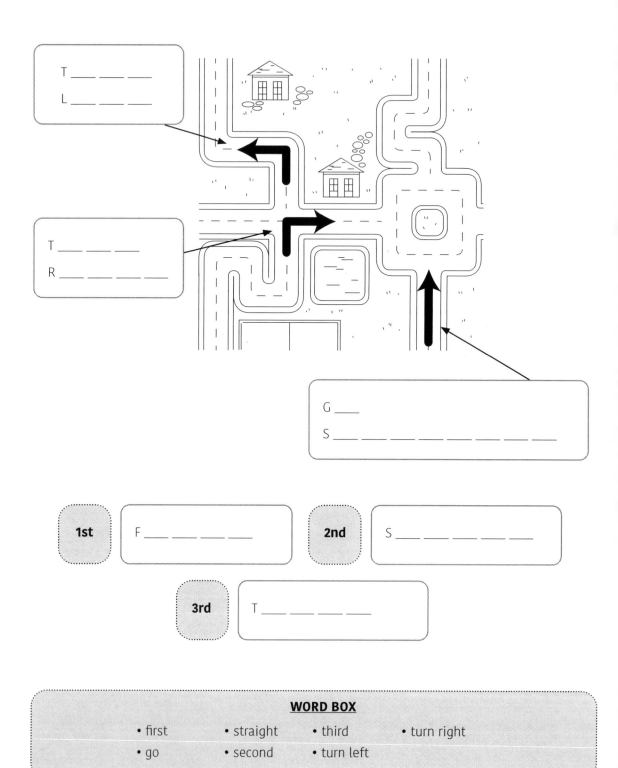

T _ _ _ _
L _ _ _ _

T _ _ _ _ _
R _ _ _ _ _ _

G _ _
S _ _ _ _ _ _ _ _ _ _

1st   F _ _ _ _ _

2nd   S _ _ _ _ _ _

3rd   T _ _ _ _ _

WORD BOX

- first
- straight
- third
- turn right
- go
- second
- turn left

Chapter 3 Directions: Fill in the blanks.

G _ _ _ _ _ _ _ _ _ _ _

G _ _ _ _ _ _ _ _ _ _ _

M _ _ _ _ _ _ _

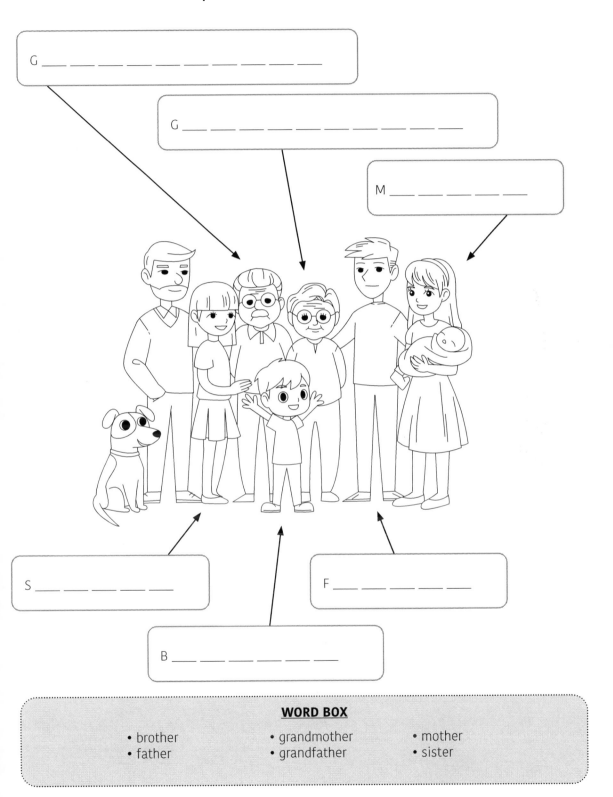

S _ _ _ _ _ _

F _ _ _ _ _ _

B _ _ _ _ _ _ _

WORD BOX

- brother
- father
- grandmother
- grandfather
- mother
- sister

B _ _ _ _ _ _ _ _ _

B _ _ _ _ _ _ _ _ _

D _ _ _ _ _ _ _

R _ _ _ _ _

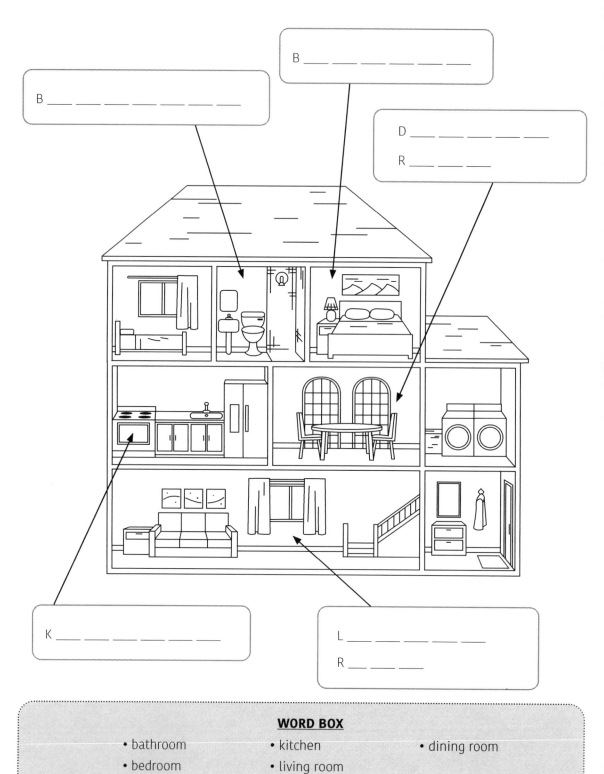

K _ _ _ _ _ _ _

L _ _ _ _ _ _

R _ _ _ _

WORD BOX

- bathroom
- bedroom
- kitchen
- living room
- dining room

Chapter 5 Directions: Fill in the blanks.

J_ __ __ __ __ __

M_ __ __ __ __

F_ __ __ __ __ __ __ __

A_ __ __ __ __

M_ __ __

J_ __ __ __ __

J_ __ __ __

S_ __ __ __ __ __ __ __ __

A_ __ __ __ __ __ __

O_ __ __ __ __ __ __

D_ __ __ __ __ __ __ __

N_ __ __ __ __ __ __ __ __

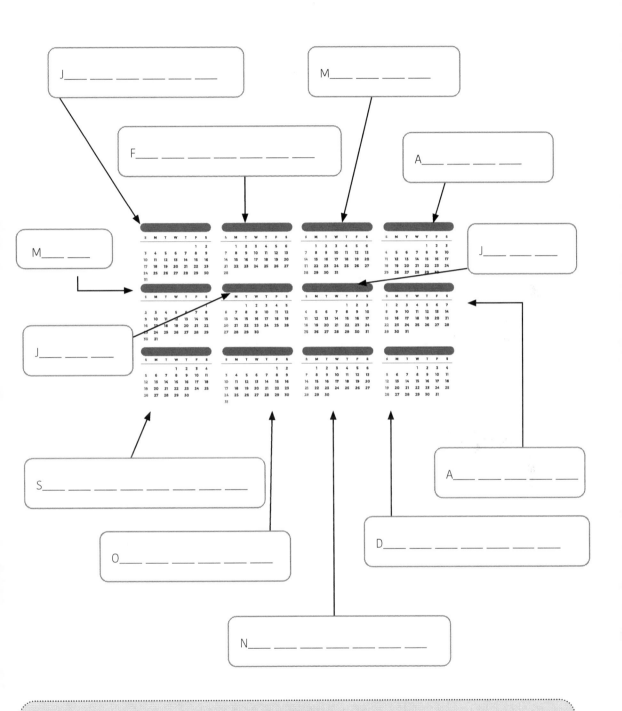

Match Directions: Match the words correctly.

1. I
2. She
3. He
4. You
5. We

A. am
B. are
C. is

9. Who
10. Where
11. When
12. What
13. Which

A. place
B. thing
C. person
D. choice between two things
E. time

14. She
15. It
16. I
17. He
18. Her
19. me
20. him

A. Myself
B. Girl or woman
C. One thing
D. Boy or man

21. Dog
22. Child
23. Pig

A. add "s"
B. add "ren"

Test

Directions: Fill in the blanks.

	WORD BOX

1. I _____ a student.

2. We _____ happy.

3. She _____ a teacher.

4. You _____ nice.

am
is
are

5. _____ is the book? The book is on the table.

6. _____ do you live? I live in this house.

7. _____ do we go to the store? We go to the store at four p.m.

8. _____ are you? I am Sam.

Who
Where
When

9. The girl is at the house. _____ is at the house.

10. I have a doll. This is _____ doll.

11. The man is nice. _____ is nice.

12. Pat has a dog. Pat has _____.

she
her
it
him
he

13. I have one _____.

14. You have two _____.

15. The mother has one _____.

16. The father has two _____.

children
child
cat
cats

17. The first month is _____.

18. The second month is _____.

19. The third month is _____.

20. The month before August is _____.

April
January
March
September
February
July

Chapter 6: HEALTH AND FEELINGS

KEY VOCABULARY WORDS AND SENTENCES

ate [āt]
Sentence: The boy ate pizza.

bone [bōn]
Sentence: My dog eats a bone.

cold [cōld]
Sentence: I have a cold.

doctor's [dŏc-tƏrs]
Sentence: I went to the doctor's office.

feel [fēl]
Sentence: I feel sick.

head [hĕd]
Sentence: My head hurts.

headache [hĕd āk]
Sentence: I have a headache.

hurt [hƏrt]
Sentence: The girls hurt their arms.

licks [lĭx]
Sentence: The dog licks its paw.

medicine [mĕd-ĭ-sĭn]
Sentence: I took some medicine.

office [ŏf – ĭs]
Sentence: You need to go to the doctor's office when you are sick.

paw [pó]
Sentence: The dog's paw is hurt.

read [rēd]
Sentence: I can read a book.

shot [shŏt]
Sentence: The nurse gave a shot.

sick [sĭk]
Sentence: The sick boy stayed home.

stomachache [stŭm – ĭk – āk]
Sentence: I have a stomachache.

took [tŭk]
Sentence: She took some pills.

well [wĕl]
Sentence: Please get well.

GRAMMAR

The subject pronoun should match its possessive adjective if a thing belongs to that pronoun. Look at the chart to show the pronouns and their matching possessive adjectives.

PRONOUN	POSSESSIVE ADJECTIVE
I	my
he	his
she	her
it	its
we	our
they	their
you	your

Look at the examples of the sentences.

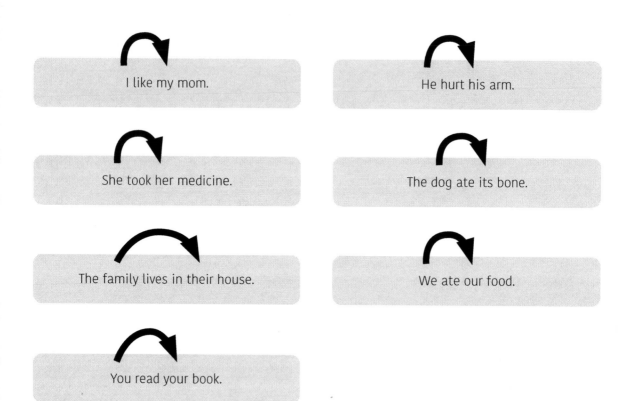

I like my mom.

He hurt his arm.

She took her medicine.

The dog ate its bone.

The family lives in their house.

We ate our food.

You read your book.

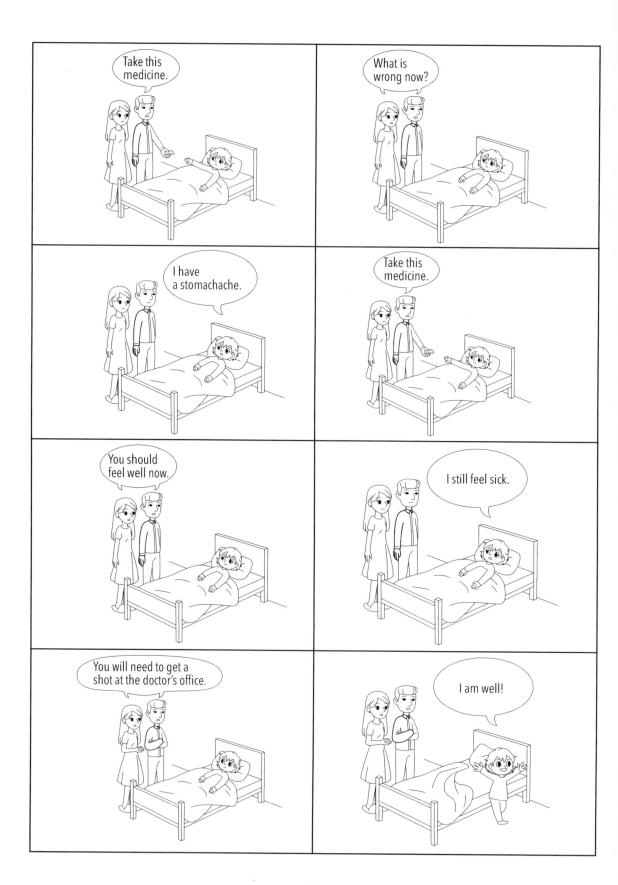

PRACTICE

Part 1 Directions: Look at the picture. Fill in the conversation.

PRACTICE

Part 2 Directions: Fill in the puzzle with the correct possessive adjective.

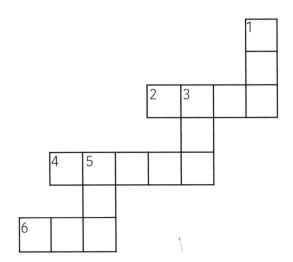

Across
2. You live with _____ sister.
4. They made _____ bed.
6. The cat licks _____ paw.

Down
1. She loves ____ dog.
3. We love _____ house.
5. The boy hurt _____ head.

Chapter 7: PARTS OF THE BODY

KEY VOCABULARY WORDS AND SENTENCES

a [ā]
    Sentence: A dog barked.

an [Ən]
    Sentence: An apple is red.

arms [ärms]
    Sentence: I hug with my arms.

clothes [clōths]
    Sentence: Put on your clothes.

ears [ērs]
    Sentence: We listen with our ears.

eyes [īz]
    Sentence: I see with my eyes.

face [fās]
    Sentence: Look at my face.

feet [fēt]
    Sentence: I put shoes on my feet.

hands [hƏnds}
    Sentence: I wave with my hands.

head [hĕd]
    Sentence: Hair is on my head.

knees [nēs]
    Sentence: I bend my knees.

legs [lĕgs]
    Sentence: I run with my legs.

mouth [maůth]
    Sentence: You speak with your mouth.

nose [nōz]
    Sentence: My nose is on my face.

shoulders [shōl – dƏrs]
    Sentence: My shoulders are
    near my arms.

snow [snō]
    Sentence: Snow is falling.

GRAMMAR

Before a noun, write "a," "an," or "the".

"A" and "an" come before any noun.
"The" comes before a certain noun.

"A" is before a noun that starts with a consonant.
"An" is before a noun that starts with a vowel.

EXAMPLES

A dog is in the yard.
(The dog is not known.)

The dog is in the yard.
(The girl knows the dog.)

An ant is in the yard.

PRACTICE

Part 1 Directions: Label the body using the words in the word box.

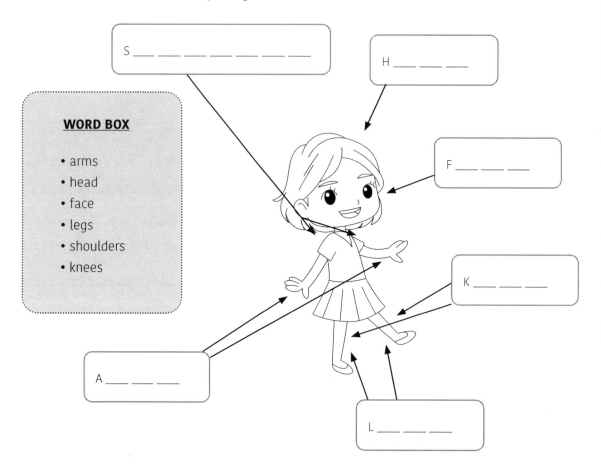

PRACTICE

Part 2 Directions: Fill in the blanks in the email with "a," "an," or "the." Note: One of the blanks is trickier than the rest!

Hi Tom!

I need _____ scarf. It is so cold outside. You have a _____.

May I use _____ scarf, please? Also, I need _____ umbrella.

It may rain today. May I use _____ umbrella at your house?

Thank you,
Sam

Chapter 8: JOBS

KEY VOCABULARY WORDS AND SENTENCES

barber [bär – bƏr]
Sentence: The barber cuts hair.

barber shop [bär – bƏr shŏp]
Sentence: The barber works at the barber shop.

blood [blŭd]
Sentence: I cut my finger and blood pours out.

boss [bŏs]
Sentence: My boss is at work.

comb [cōm]
Sentence: Comb your hair.

danger [dān - jƏr]
Sentence: Danger is ahead.

dentist [dĭn – tĭst]
Sentence: The dentist cleans my teeth.

doctor [dŏk – tƏr]
Sentence: The doctor helps people.

fights [fĭts]
Sentence: The kids fight.

guts [gŭts]
Sentence: His guts were showing.

hair [hār]
Sentence: I need to cut my hair.

haircut [hār – cŭt]
Sentence: I need a haircut.

health [hĕlth]
Sentence: My health is good.

hospital [hŏs – pĭt – Əl]
Sentence: Sick people go to the hospital.

learn [lƏrn]
Sentence: Children learn to read.

nurse [nƏrs]
Sentence: The nurse is at the hospital.

policeman [pō – lēs – man]
Sentence: The policeman helps us.

police officer [pō – lēs ŏf – ĭ – sƏr]
Sentence: The police officer stood at the corner.

police station [pō – lēs stā – shŭn]
Sentence: The police are at the police station.

pretty [prĭt – ē]
Sentence: The girl is pretty.

read [rēd]
Sentence: I read a book.

school [skül]
Sentence: I go to school.

teacher [tēch – Ər]
Sentence: The teacher teaches.

GRAMMAR

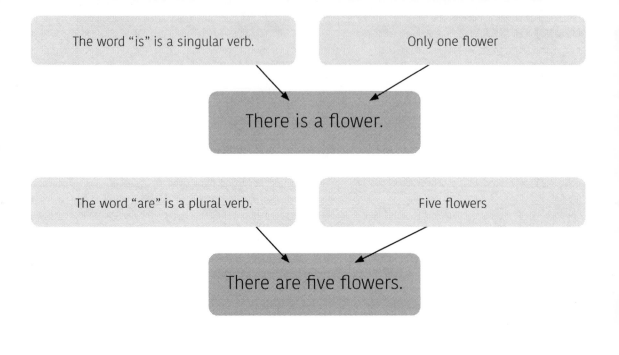

"There is" and "There are" = look at the rest of the sentence.

The word "is" is a singular verb.

Only one flower

There is a flower.

The word "are" is a plural verb.

Five flowers

There are five flowers.

EXAMPLE SENTENCES

Directions: Read the sentences.

1. There are three children in the street.
2. There is a tree in the yard.
3. There are dogs barking.
4. There is one teacher.
5. There are no books on the table.

PRACTICE

Part 1 Directions: Read each activity. Think about things you like. Check the box next to something you like.

☐	1. Danger	☐	6. Breaking up fights
☐	2. Taking care of yourself	☐	7. Being the boss
☐	3. Combing hair	☐	8. Reading
☐	4. Learning	☐	9. Blood and gut
☐	5. Looking pretty	☐	10. Children

Directions: From the list that you checked, circle the numbers next to the jobs.
Find the job that has the most circled numbers.

JOBS

Barber – 2, 3, 5, 12, 15

Teacher – 4, 8, 10, 13, 15

Nurse – 2, 9, 11, 15

PRACTICE

Part 2 Directions: Unscramble the sentences.

a is nice policeman there

are boats in the there water

are ground in plants the there

are five flowers there

a in is sky star the there

are doctors five hospital in the there

a boy house in is the there

are in my notebook papers some there

Chapter 9: LIKES AND DISLIKES

KEY VOCABULARY WORDS AND SENTENCES

binders [bīn – dər s]
Sentence: Binders hold paper.

books [bŭks]
Sentence: I opened the book.

clipboard [clip - bȯrd]
Sentence: The paper is on a clipboard.

close [clōz]
Sentence: Close the door.

computer [kəm - pyü – tər]
Sentence: I typed on the computer.

dance [däns]
Sentence: We dance together.

dislike [dĭs – līk]
Sentence: I dislike pizza.

dress [drĕs]
Sentence: I wore a dress.

envelopes [ĭn – vĕl – ōps]
Sentence: I put the letter in the envelope.

far [fär]
Sentence: Do not go far.

fish [fĭsh]
Sentence: Fish swim in ponds.

French fries [frĭnch frīz]
Sentence: I eat french fries.

hamburger [ham – bər – gər]
Sentence: I ate a hamburger.

hotdog [hŏt – dŏg]
Sentence: I like hotdogs.

hate [hāt]
Sentence: I hate soup.

like [līk]
Sentence: I like food.

paper [pā – pər]
Sentence: I write on paper.

pencil [pĭn – səl]
Sentence: I write with a pencil.

phone [fōn]
Sentence: Answer the phone.

pizza [pēt – zə]
Sentence: I eat pizza.

sandwich [sand – wĭch]
Sentence: I made a sandwich.

that [that]
Sentence: Look at that dog.

these [thēz]
Sentence: Look at these dogs.

this [this]
Sentence: Look at this dog.

those [thōz]
Sentence: Look at those dogs.

GRAMMAR

Use THIS, THAT, THESE, and THOSE to show things that are near or far to you.

Look at the pictures to show which word to use.

Look at this dog.

Close and one dog

Look at that dog.

Far and one dog

Look at these dogs.

Close and more than one dog

Look at those dogs.

Far and more than one dog

PRACTICE

Part 1 Directions: Write three complete sentences about what you like and what you don't like on the menu.

MENU

Hamburger

Pizza

Fish

French Fries

Sandwich

Hotdog

PRACTICE

Part 2 Directions: Describe the picture by filling in the blanks with things found in the picture. Think about how close or far away the things are from the woman.

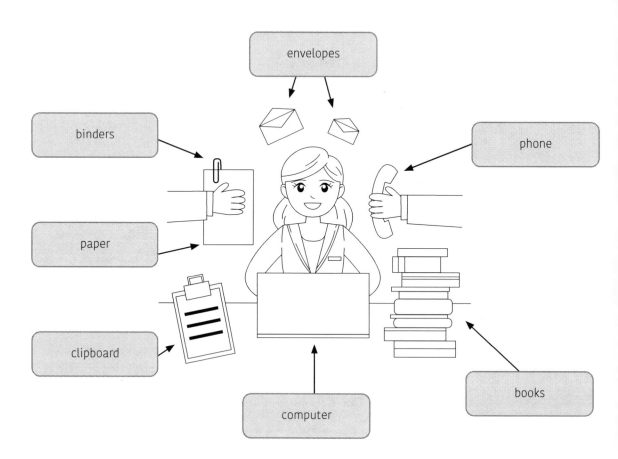

This _____

That _____

These _____

Those _____

Chapter 10: PAST EVENTS

KEY VOCABULARY WORDS AND SENTENCES

ago [ə – gō]
Sentence: I worked 2 days ago.

asked [ăskt]
Sentence: I asked a question.

birth [bərth]
Sentence: My birth was in May.

burned [bərnd]
Sentence: I burned a candle.

candle [kan – dəl]
Sentence: The candle was on the table.

carried [ker – ēd]
Sentence: I carried a book.

cleaned [clēnd]
Sentence: I cleaned my house.

cooked [kůkd]
Sentence: Mom cooked a meal.

dressed [drĕsd]
Sentence: I dressed in a shirt.

driving [drī-ving]
Sentence: I was driving my car.

kicked [kĭkd]
Sentence: I kicked a ball.

marry [mā -rē]
Sentence: The man will marry his wife.

practice [prăk – tĭs]
Sentence: We will practice the sport.

pulled [pəld]
Sentence: I pulled a rope.

purchase [pər – chĭs]
Sentence: I will purchase a book.

thanked [thangkd]
Sentence: We thanked the man.

walked [wȯkd]
Sentence: I walked to the store.

worked [wərkd]
Sentence: I worked all day.

yesterday [yĕs – tər – dā]
Sentence: I went to the mall yesterday.

GRAMMAR

A verb in the past tense sometimes ends in "ed."

Add "ed" to most verbs to make them past tense

Read the examples.

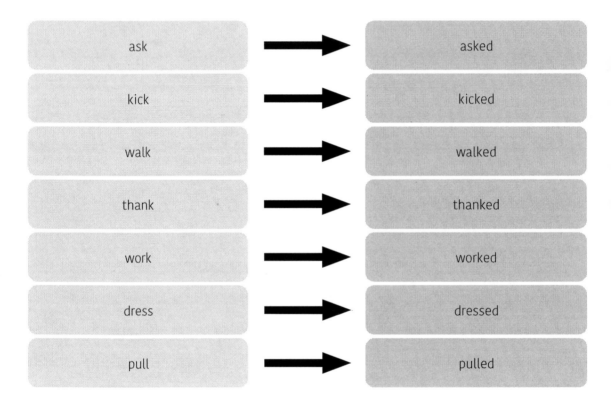

ask	asked
kick	kicked
walk	walked
thank	thanked
work	worked
dress	dressed
pull	pulled

Read the sentences.

1. I dressed myself this morning.
2. The man worked all day.
3. The boy kicked the ball in the game.
4. The students asked the questions during class.
5. I walked two miles last week.

PRACTICE

Part 1 Directions: Write a sentence about something important you did during each time.

Yesterday	....
Three days ago	....
Last week	....
Last year	....
Five years ago	....

PRACTICE

Part 2 Directions: Think about your own life. Sort the events in the box into Past, Present, or Never Happened. Then write the verb correctly in the correct category.

- learn to read
- marry
- start school
- play a sport
- work at a job
- practice driving
- birth a child
- finish school
- purchase a house

PAST	PRESENT	NEVER HAPPENED

Review and Advancement for Chapters 6 through 10

Chapter 6 Vocabulary Directions: Match the picture to the word. Write the letter in the blank.

_____ 1. doctor

_____ 2. headache

_____ 3. cold

_____ 4. bone

_____ 5. paw

_____ 6. shot

_____ 7. medicine

_____ 8. stomachache

A.

B.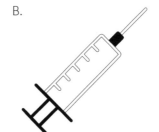

C.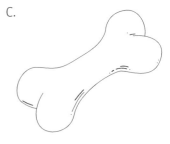

D.

E.

F.

G.

H.

Chapter 7 Vocabulary Directions: Read the story. The fill in the blank with the correct word from the word box. You will not use all of the words.

- arms
- ears
- hands

- head
- knees
- legs

- mouth
- nose
- shoulders

- eyes
- face

Sarah saw a dog down the road. She sees with her _____. Then she smelled a rose. She smells with her _____. She found a dog. The dog ate food. The dog eats with his

_____.

Sarah fell over the dog. She fell onto her _____. Blood dripped down her _____. Then her mother called to her. She heard her mother with her _____. The mother put her _____ on Sarah's wound. That stopped the bleeding.

Chapter 8 Vocabulary Directions: Read the clues for each job. Write the job, or the person who does that job, on the line.

1. _____

teeth

brush

tool

2. _____

learn

school

kids

3. _____

hair

cut

style

4. _____

help people

crime

handcuffs

5. _____

give shots

medicine

care

Chapter 9 Vocabulary Directions: Write a sentence about each thing and say whether you like it or dislike it

Do you like or dislike this?

1. Eating a hamburger

_____

2. Eating a Pizza

_____

3. Talking on the phone

_____

4. Playing on the computer

_____

5. Dancing

_____

6. Reading a book

_____

Chapter 10 Vocabulary Directions: Fill in the blank with the correct verb in the past tense.

- burned
- carried
- cleaned
- cooked
- dressed
- kicked
- pulled
- thanked
- walked

1. My mom gave me a present this morning. I _____ her.

2. A fire _____ my dress.

3. The player _____ the ball in the game.

4. The girl _____ weeds out of the garden.

5. I got _____ this morning. I put on clothes.

6. My mom _____ our house. Now it is beautiful.

7. My father _____ dinner. He made steak and potatoes.

8. We _____ to the store because it is close by.

9. Then we _____ the food home from the store.

GRAMMAR PRACTICE

Part 1 Directions: Fill in the blank with the correct possessive adjective. It should match the subject.

She walked _____ dog.

The dog dug _____ hole.

I love _____ dog.

He ate _____ pizza.

They talked on _____ phones.

You like _____ dress.

The ant carried _____ food.

I ate _____ food.

We followed _____ children.

They ran to _____ schools.

You want _____ cake.

I like _____ book.

He asked _____ question.

They sat on _____ steps.

We looked at _____ shoes.

You did _____ work.

She did _____ homework.

The cat licked _____ paw.

He loves _____ hair.

She called _____ friend.

We drove to _____ house.

GRAMMAR PRACTICE

Part 2 Directions: Match the articles to the correct sentence.

A. a   **B**. an   **C**. the

1. _____ yellow dog crossed the road.

2. _____ flower is in a field.

3. _____ egg is on the table.

4. I see _____ boys outside.

5. My mom looked for _____ sugar.

6. I will eat _____ orange from the six oranges in the bowl.

7. She will go to _____ store on the corner.

8. Karen likes to go to _____ beach near her house.

9. We will go to _____ park next week.

10. I will cook _____ pizzas for dinner.

11. Sarah puts on _____ watch from her mother.

12. _____ cat chased our dog. I don't know that cat.

GRAMMAR PRACTICE

Part 3 Directions: Unscramble the sentences. Then write them in the correct order.

1. books table there the are on two

_____

2. my there chair in is

_____

3. bed a there the pillow is on

_____

4. park children are at there the four

_____

5. apple bowl in is an the there

_____

6. backyard dogs are the there in

_____

7. a on chair cat the is there

_____

8. house three there in the are beds

_____

9. are doctors hospital the there in many

_____

10. ice an cone cream there

_____

GRAMMAR PRACTICE

Part 4 Directions: Draw the picture as described. Then write a sentence using "this," "that," "these," or "those."

1. Draw a picture of yourself with three flowers near you.

2. Draw a picture of yourself with one flower far away from you.

3. Draw a picture of yourself with one flower near you.

4. Draw a picture of yourself with three flowers far away from you.

GRAMMAR PRACTICE

Part 5 Directions: Read each sentence. Underline the verb in each sentence. Then write the verb in the past tense.

1. Tim thanks his friend for the present.

Verb in the past tense: _____

2. The food burns on the stove.

Verb in the past tense: _____

3. The maid cleans the house.

Verb in the past tense: _____

4. The little girl dresses her doll.

Verb in the past tense: _____

5. Most people walk to work.

Verb in the past tense: _____

6. The woman carries flowers in her hands.

Verb in the past tense: _____

7. The man cooks food.

Verb in the past tense: _____

8. I kick the ball across the field.

Verb in the past tense: _____

9. She pulls the table over to the wall.

Verb in the past tense: _____

Test: Chapters Six through Ten

Part 1 Directions: Choose the correct vocabulary word from Chapters Six through Ten to fill in the blank.

1. The dog licked its _____.

2. The nurse gave me a _____ in my arm.

3. I ate something bad, so I have a _____.

4. The _____ gave me some medicine.

5. I broke a _____ in my leg.

6. I opened my _____ to sing.

7. At night, I close my _____ to sleep.

8. I use my _____ to hear the music.

9. I run with my _____.

10. I hug my friends with my _____.

11. The _____ cuts hair.

12. The _____ helps students learn.

13. The sick people go to the _____.

14. The _____ stopped the bad man.

15. The _____ pulled a tooth.

16. I read many _____.

17. I type on a _____.

18. I talk to my friends on a _____.

19. I ate a _____ on a bun.

20. I put lettuce and tomato on my _____.

21. The fire _____ in the fireplace.

22. The beans _____ in the pot.

23. We _____ weeds in the yard.

24. My brother is mean. He _____ me.

25. I _____ my room and picked up my clothes.

Part 2 Directions: Read each question. Circle the correct answer from the choices.

1. She likes _____ own hair.

    A. your   **B**. our   **C**. its   **D**. her

2. I like _____ dress.

    A. its   **B**. our   **C**. she   **D.** my

3. He wants to find _____ shoes.

    A. its   **B**. his   **C**. mine   **D**. you

4. They saw _____ friends at school.

    A. its   **B**. their   **C.** him   **D.** he

5. You must know _____ phone number.

    A. your   **B**. you   **C.** she   **D**. he

6. _____ lamp is on this table.

    A. A   **B**. An   **C**. The

7. _____ shirts are in the closet.

    A. A   **B**. An   **C**. The

8. _____ apple is red or green.

    A. A   **B**. An   **C**. The

9. We walked to _____ friend's store.

    A. a   **B**. an   **C.** the

10. Somewhere, _____ store is closed.

    A. a   **B**. an   **C**. the

11. _____ a star in the sky.

    A. There is   **B**. There are

12. _____ three rings.

    A. There is   **B**. There are

13. _____many children.

    A. There is   **B**. There are

14._____ a door in the wall.

    A. There is   **B**. There are

15._____ four dogs.

    A. There is   **B**. There are

16. I am holding _____ flower in my hand.

    A. this   **B**. that   **C.** these   **D.** those

17. I am holding _____ flowers in my hands.

    A. this   **B**. that   **C**. these   **D**. those

18. She is holding _____ flower. She is across the room.

   A. this   **B**. that   **C**. these   **D**. those

19. She is holding _____ flowers. She is across the room.

   A. this   **B**. that   **C**. these   **D**. those

20. She is holding _____ flower. She is standing next to me.

   A. this   **B**. that   **C**. these   **D**. those

21. She _____ the table with a rag.

   A. burned   **B**. cleaned   **C**. carried   **D**. pulled

22. The cook _____ the food. No one ate it.

   A. cooked   **B**. kicked   **C**. walked   **D**. burned

23. We _____ the ball.

   A. dressed   **B**. pulled   **C**. kicked   **D**. thanked

24. The boy _____ the heavy books.

   A. pulled   **B**. carried   **C**. burned   **D**. walked

25. The man _____ the rope up.

   A. pulled   **B**. cooked   **C**. kicked   **D**. thanked

Chapter 11: SPORTS

KEY VOCABULARY WORDS AND SENTENCES

ball [bŏl]
Sentence: The girl catches the ball.

baseball [bās bŏl]
Sentence: We play baseball.

basketball [bās kĕt bŏl]
Sentence: You throw the ball into a hoop in basketball.

bat [băt]
Sentence: You swing the bat around.

court [kȯrt]
Sentence: You play basketball on a court.

dribble [drĭb Əl]
Sentence: Dribble the ball.

field [fēld]
Sentence: Football is played on a field.

football [fūt bŏl]
Sentence: I play football.

hockey [hŏk ē]
Sentence: Hockey is played on ice.

home run [hōm rŭn]
Sentence: Hit a home run in baseball.

hoop [hoop]
Sentence: Throw the ball into the hoop.

kick [kĭk]
Sentence: Kick the football.

puck [pŭk]
Sentence: Shoot the puck into the net.

run [rŭn]
Sentence: Run down the field.

shoot [shūt]
Sentence: Shoot the ball.

skates [skāts]
Sentence: You need skates to play hockey.

stick [stĭk]
Sentence: You also need a stick to play hockey.

swing [swēng]
Sentence: Swing the bat.

tackle [tăk Əl]
Sentence: You tackle players in football.

touchdown [tŭch daủn]
Sentence: Score a touchdown in football.

yards [yärdz]
Sentence: Run many yards in football.

GRAMMAR

Singular verbs in the present tense – end in "s"

Plural verbs in the present tense – do NOT end in "s"

1. Identify the subject. Is the subject singular or plural?

EXAMPLES

The girl <u>eats</u> cake.

One girl = verb + "s"

Read the sentences. Look for the subject and verb. See if they match. Are they both singular or both plural?

1. The dogs bark at the cat.

2. The cat meows at the dog.

3. A child yells at his sister.

4. My sister tells our mom.

5. A mom walks to the store.

6. Two students write on their papers.

7. Six men read books.

8. The children paint pictures.

9. Birds fly in the sky.

10. A man drives a car.

11. Teachers grade papers.

12. A barber cuts hair.

13. Four nurses give shots.

14. Karen eats food.

15. The door opens.

16. Molly talks to her son.

17. Sarah watches TV.

18. The girl sits in a chair.

19. The maid cleans.

20. She dresses in a skirt.

PRACTICE

Part 1 Directions: Fill in the blanks of the text conversation. Write in the present tense. Watch for correct subject-verb agreement.

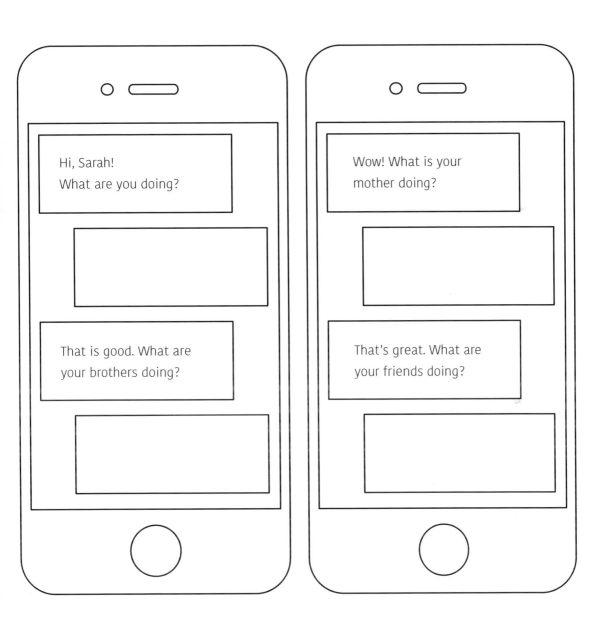

Hi, Sarah!
What are you doing?

That is good. What are your brothers doing?

Wow! What is your mother doing?

That's great. What are your friends doing?

PRACTICE

Part 2 Directions: Read the poems below. Write down the sport that is described in each poem.

1. _____

> With the ball in my hands
> Dribble, dribble down the court
> Throw the ball in the hoop
> I really love this sport

2. _____

> With a stick and a puck
> I skate down the ice
> Score a goal into the net
> This would be really nice.

3. _____

> Bases, a ball, and a bat
> Is all I really need
> Make a home run
> This is good indeed.

4. _____

> Running many, many yards
> Down the field with the ball
> Players tackle each other
> A touchdown and all.

PRACTICE

Part 3 Directions: Fill in the blank with a correct verb. Think of a verb that would make sense. Think about subject-verb agreement.

1. People _____ with their eyes.

2. Basketball players _____ balls into the hoops.

3. A baseball player _____ the ball.

4. He _____ the bases in a baseball game.

5. The hockey player _____ down the ice.

6. Two rabbits _____ in the grass.

7. The baby _____ in his crib.

8. My dad _____ video games.

9. A doctor _____ medicine.

10. The girls _____ their teeth.

PRACTICE

Part 4 Directions: Read the story. Then answer the questions in complete sentences.

Tim wants to play a sport. He doesn't know which sport. Does he want to play soccer? He thinks for a minute. He likes to kick balls. He does not like to run outside.

Then Tim plays basketball. That sport is inside. He dribbles the ball down the court. He shoots the ball. It drops through the hoop. He likes basketball, but he will try other sports.

Next, Tim goes to the baseball field. He picks up a bat. The pitcher throws the ball to Tim. Tim swings the bat around. He misses. He misses again. Tim does not like baseball.

Last, Tim puts on his skates. He skates around the rink. He falls down again and again. He does not like hockey.

Tim plays basketball.

1. What sport does Tim play first?

_____

2. What sport does Tim like?

_____

3. What happens at the rink?

_____

4. Where does Tim play baseball?

_____

5. When does Tim play basketball?

_____

Chapter 12: CLOTHING

KEY VOCABULARY WORDS AND SENTENCES

box [bŏks]
  Sentence: Put the clothes in the box.

clothes [klōz]
  Sentence: We wear clothes.

dress [drĕs]
  Sentence: She wore a long dress.

how many [haů mĭ nē]
  Sentence: How many TVs do you have?

how much [haů mӘch]
  Sentence: How much does it cost?

move [moov]
  Sentence: We are going to move.

moving [moov ing]
  Sentence: We are moving to the city.

pants [pants]
  Sentence: Girls and boys wear pants.

shirts [shӘrts]
  Sentence: There are twenty-two shirts in the store.

shoes [shoos]
  Sentence: Put on your shoes.

shorts [shȯrts]
  Sentence: I wear shorts in the summer.

socks [sŏx]
  Sentence: I put socks on my feet.

sweater [swĕt Әr]
  Sentence: I wear a sweater in the winter.

GRAMMAR

*Use "how much" when something can't be counted and can only be measured.

*Use "how many" when something can be counted.

EXAMPLES

*How many marbles are in the jar?
You can count them.
There are two hundred marbles in the jar.

*How many people are in line?
You can count them.
There are five people in line.

*How much juice is in the glass?
It can be measured.
There are two cups of juice in the glass.

*How much does this watch cost?
It costs money.
This watch costs $10.

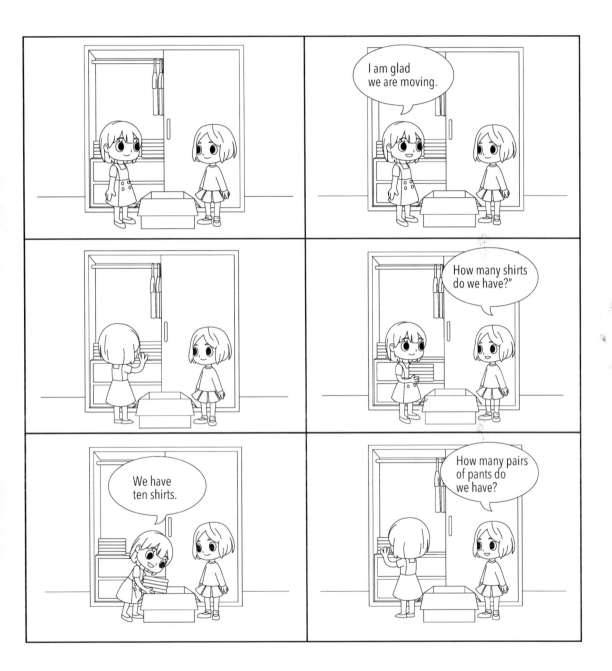

PRACTICE

Part 1 Directions: Guess how much or how many of something.

1. How many candies are in the jar? _____

2. How much does this diamond ring cost? _____

3. How much water is in the cup? _____

PRACTICE

Part 2 Directions: In the grey spaces, write what you would ask the store clerk.

This purple dress costs $25.

The red dress costs $17.

We have four dresses.

There are twelve pairs of pants.

PRACTICE

Part 3 Directions: Answer the questions about yourself.

ALL ABOUT YOURSELF

1. How many brothers do you have?

_____

2. How much do you love your parents?

_____

3. How many pets do you own?

_____

4. How much money do you have?

_____

PRACTICE

Part 4 Directions: Read the story and look at the picture. Then answer the questions.

Sam goes to the store. He buys many things. He buys three types of meat. He will make fish for dinner tonight. He buys steak, fish, and turkey. Then he goes to the vegetable area. He buys bananas, carrots, and apples. Then Sam goes to buy milk. His children drink a lot of milk, so he needs to buy a lot more milk. He buys wine for his wife and himself. They drink wine at dinner and sometimes after dinner. Lastly, Sam buys some cheese. His children like to eat cheese sandwiches.

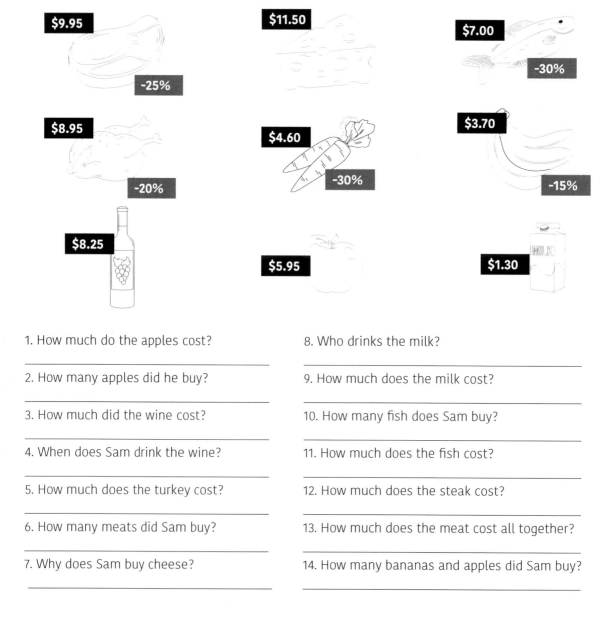

$9.95   -25%

$11.50

$7.00   -30%

$8.95   -20%

$4.60   -30%

$3.70   -15%

$8.25

$5.95

$1.30

1. How much do the apples cost?

2. How many apples did he buy?

3. How much did the wine cost?

4. When does Sam drink the wine?

5. How much does the turkey cost?

6. How many meats did Sam buy?

7. Why does Sam buy cheese?

8. Who drinks the milk?

9. How much does the milk cost?

10. How many fish does Sam buy?

11. How much does the fish cost?

12. How much does the steak cost?

13. How much does the meat cost all together?

14. How many bananas and apples did Sam buy?

Chapter 13: TRANSPORTATION

KEY VOCABULARY WORDS AND SENTENCES

airplane [er plan]
Sentence: The airplane took off.

airport [er pƏrt]
Sentence: The airplane is at
the airport.

at [ăt]
Sentence: She is at school.

atop [ŭ tŏp]
Sentence: The ball is atop the box.

bus [bŭs]
Sentence: We ride the bus to school.

drives [drīvs]
Sentence: My mom drives a car.

flies [flīz]
Sentence: An airplane flies in the sky.

in [ĭn]
Sentence: The ball is in the box.

inside [ĭn sīd]
Sentence: The people are inside
the airport.

next to [nĕxt too]
Sentence: The ball is next to the box.

object [ŏb jĕkt]
Sentence: This is an object.

on [ŏn]
Sentence: The ball is on the box.

out [aŭt]
Sentence: We went out the door.

outside [aŭt sīd]
Sentence: The tree is outside.

parking lot [pärk ing lŏt]
Sentence: The cars are in the parking
lot.

railroad [rāl rōd]
Sentence: The train runs on a railroad.

rolling [rōl ing]
Sentence: The ball is rolling on
the ground.

runway [rŭn wāy]
Sentence: The airplane is on
the runway.

sandbox [sand bŏks]
Sentence: We play in the sandbox.

to [too]
Sentence: We went to the store.

tracks [trăks]
Sentence: Trains ride on tracks.

train [trān]
Sentence: We rode the train.

transportation [trans pƏr tā shƏn]
Sentence: Cars are transportation.

zoo [zoo]
Sentence: Animals live in a zoo.

GRAMMAR

COMMON PREPOSITIONS

Common prepositions are IN, AT, ON, TO, and OUT.
Look at the pictures below and read the sentences.
1. The ball is in the box.
2. The ball is at the box.
3. The ball is on the box.
4. The ball is out of the box.
5. The ball is rolling to the box

In the box   **On** the box   **Out of** the box

So, the meanings of the prepositions are:

*in – inside
*at - next to
*on – sitting atop of
*to – moving toward
*out - outside

Read the sentences below. Think of the meaning of the preposition. Then think of a picture of that sentence.

1. The kitchen is in the house.

2. The fans are at the game.

3. The book is on the table.

4. We are going to the store.

5. The money is out of the purse.

6. Stan is in his room.

7. The children are at the birthday party.

8. The car is on the road.

9. The teens are going to the movies.

10. The ice fell out of the glass.

PRACTICE

Part 1 Directions: Look at each picture. Read about the transportation. Then answer the question.

1. This transportation flies around the world. You can see it in the sky. It lands on a runway at the airport. What is it?

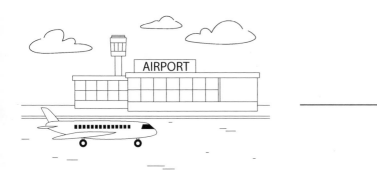

_____

2. This transportation drives on roads. They park in parking lots. Many people drive this transportation to work and then back home. What is it?

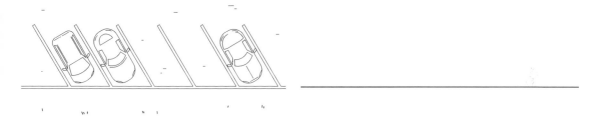

_____

3. This transportation is on tracks. You may see a railroad station. People ride this transportation to get out of a city. What is it?

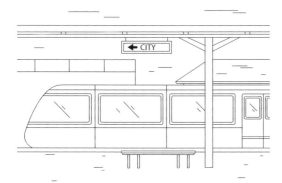

_____

PRACTICE

Part 2 Directions: Look at the picture. Read each clue. Then guess the object in the picture from the clue.

1. _____

Clue 1: This object is red.

Clue 2: It is rolling to a boy.

Clue 3: It is on the ground.

2. _____

Clue 1: Someone built this object.

Clue 2: The object is in a box.

Clue 3: A flag is on this object.

3. _____

Clue 1: It is on the ground.

Clue 2: It is running to the sandbox.

Clue 3: It is out of the sandbox.

PRACTICE

Part 3 Directions: Read the email. Then write a few sentences below responding to the email.

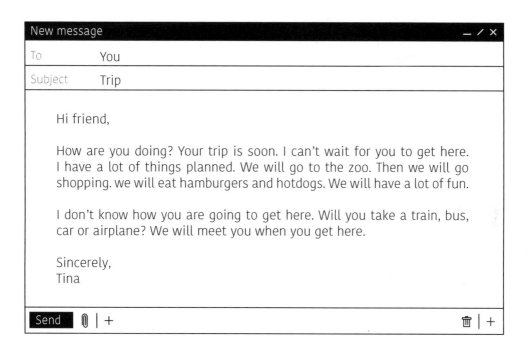

New message — ╱ ✕

To You

Subject Trip

Hi friend,

How are you doing? Your trip is soon. I can't wait for you to get here. I have a lot of things planned. We will go to the zoo. Then we will go shopping. we will eat hamburgers and hotdogs. We will have a lot of fun.

I don't know how you are going to get here. Will you take a train, bus, car or airplane? We will meet you when you get here.

Sincerely,
Tina

Send 🖉 | +   🗑 | +

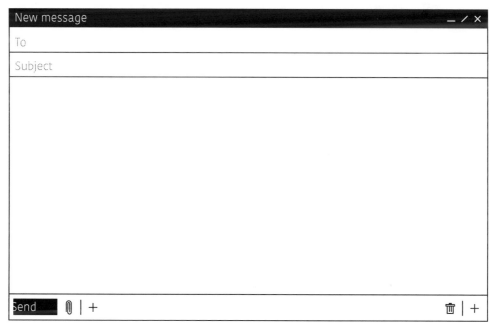

New message — ╱ ✕

To

Subject

Send 🖉 | +   🗑 | +

PRACTICE

Part 4 Directions: Answer these questions about yourself. Write them in complete sentences.

TRANSPORTATION AND ME

1. Do you ride in a car to school?

2. When do you ride a bus?

3. Have you ever been in an airplane?

4. Where do you go to fly in an airplane?

5. Do you have a train in your city?

6. When do you fly in an airplane?

7. Are trains fast or slow?

8. Do airplanes fly in the sky?

9. How many airplanes have you seen?

10. How many cars does your family have?

Chapter 14: HOBBIES

KEY VOCABULARY WORDS AND SENTENCES

blankets [blank ĕts]
Sentence: Cover me with blankets.

counted [kaůnt ĕd]
Sentence: We counted the stars.

favorite [fāv ∂r ĭt]
Sentence: My favorite color is blue.

friendship [frĭnd shĭp]
Sentence: Friendship is important.

listen [lĭs ĭn]
Sentence: Listen to your teacher.

music [mū zĭk]
Sentence: I like to listen to music.

pillows [pĭl lōs]
Sentence: Pillows are on my bed.

play [plā]
Sentence: Play with your toys.

sports [sp∂rtz]
Sentence: Some people like to play sports.

television [tĕl ĭ vĭ zhŭn]
Sentence: I like to watch television.

video games [vĭd ē ō gāmz]
Sentence: Many children like to play video games.

watch [wŏch]
Sentence: People watch movies.

GRAMMAR

USING "MUCH," "MANY," AND "A LOT" IN SENTENCES (AND NOT QUESTIONS)

* Use "much" when something can't be counted.
* Use "many" when something can be counted.
* Use "a lot" when something can or can't be counted.
** Remember "a lot" is two words.

READ THE EXAMPLES BELOW AND THINK ABOUT WHETHER THOSE THINGS CAN BE COUNTED OR NOT.

1. Thank you so much!

2. I love him so much!

3. There is so much to be thankful for.

4. I have many friends.

5. There are many flowers in the garden.

6. Many people walk down the street.

7. The girl has a lot of homework to do.

8. We have a lot of presents.

9. I like that idea a lot.

PRACTICE

Part 1 Directions: Choose whether or not these things can be counted. Circle the word. Then write a sentence with "much," "many," or "a lot."

1. Blankets

    Can you count this? YES   NO

    Write a sentence: _____

2. Friendship

    Can you count this? YES   NO

    Write a sentence: _____

3. Dogs

    Can you count this? YES   NO

    Write a sentence: _____

4. Pillows

    Can you count this? YES   NO

    Write a sentence: _____

5. Love

    Can you count this? YES   NO

    Write a sentence: _____

6. Books

    Can you count this? YES   NO

    Write a sentence: _____

7. Happiness

    Can you count this? YES   NO

    Write a sentence: _____

PRACTICE

Part 2 Directions: Read each paragraph. What hobby is it? Write it on the line.

1. People run in this hobby. This hobby includes basketball, hockey, and baseball. Most people need a ball or something else to play this. What hobby is it?

_____

2. It does not take much to do this hobby. This hobby is found in most homes. People turn it on and watch it. Then they sit for a long time. What hobby is it?

_____

3. People will not talk during this hobby. They will put something in their ears. Then they will turn it on. Some people will use their phones for this hobby. Then they listen. What hobby is it?

_____

4. This hobby is sometimes found on the phone. People play these a lot. Sometimes, parents have to stop their children from this hobby. It is a lot of fun. What hobby is it?

_____

5. People need to be quiet to do this hobby. They may do this hobby in their room. Some people go to a library first. What hobby is it?

_____

PRACTICE

Part 3 Directions: Answer the questions.

1. What hobby is usually done outside?
    A. television
    B. baseball
    C. books
    D. video games

2. What do you do when you want to watch TV?
    A. run
    B. play it
    C. listen to it
    D. turn it on

3. What do you need to listen to music?
    A. ball
    B. television
    C. phone
    D. sport

4. What do you do with a video game?
    A. run it
    B. watch it
    C. turn it
    D. play it

5. When do teenagers usually play sports?
    A. in the morning
    B. after school
    C. during math class
    D. in the middle of the night

6. Why do parents stop children from playing video games?
    A. Because they play too much
    B. Because they don't play enough
    C. Because they play a little
    D. Because they are fun

PRACTICE

Part 4 Directions: Answer each question about you and that hobby.

1. BASKETBALL

    Do you like to watch basketball on television? _____

    Do you play basketball with your friends? _____

    Is there a video game about basketball? _____

2. WATCH TELEVISION

    How much television do you watch? _____

    What do you watch on television? _____

    Where is your television? _____

3. VIDEO GAMES

    What is your favorite video game? _____

    How many video games do you have? _____

    How much time do you spend playing video games? _____

4. READING BOOKS

    Do you like to read books? _____

    What is your favorite book? _____

    Where do you get your books? _____

5. LISTENING TO MUSIC

    How do you listen to music? _____

    When do you listen to music? _____

    What music do you listen to? _____

Chapter 15: FOOD

KEY VOCABULARY WORDS AND SENTENCES

buns [bŭnz]
   Sentence: Hot dogs are on buns.

cake [cāk}
   Sentence: I like to eat cake.

can [can]
   Sentence: I can do math.

cheese [chēz]
   Sentence: I like cheese pizza.

chips [chips]
   Sentence: I eat potato chips.

delicious [dē lĭsh ŭs]
   Sentence: Cake is delicious.

dessert [dĭ zƏrt]
   Sentence: Eat dessert after dinner.

drink [drēnk]
   Sentence: I drink water.

hamburger [ham bƏr gƏr]
   Sentence: I like to eat hamburgers.

hot dogs [hŏt dŏgz]
   Sentence: Hot dogs are great.

may [mā]
   Sentence: May I play video games?

might [mīt]
   Sentence: We might go outside.

order [ȯr dƏr]
   Sentence: Order your food.

pasta [pŏ stƏ]
   Sentence: Pasta is good.

pizza [pē zƏ]
   Sentence: Pizza is hot.

potatoes [pō tā tōz]
   Sentence: Eat your potatoes.

sauce [sŏs]
   Sentence: Spaghetti has sauce on it.

server [sƏr vƏr]
   Sentence: The server came to
   our table.

sides [sīdz]
   Sentence: Your hamburger
   comes with two sides.

spaghetti [spŏ gĕt tē]
   Sentence: Spaghetti is pasta.

GRAMMAR

" Can," "may" and "might" are used a lot. They have different meanings. They should be used in different ways.

* Can means that you are able to do something
* May means that you are allowed to do something
* Might means that it is possible for you to do something

Read the sentences. Think about what each sentence means.

1. Sarah can ride a bike. She puts her feet on the pedals. Then she moves the pedals up and down. The bike moves forward.

2. Sarah may ride her bike. Her mother said she could. She asked her mother and her mom said, "Yes."

3. Sarah might ride her bike. She might do something else. She might play with her friends. She does not know yet.

PRACTICE

Part 1 Directions: Read the conversation. Fill in the blanks with the correct words.

Server: Hi, what would you like to drink?

You: _____

Server: Would you like to order now?

You: _____

Server: What would you like to order?

You: _____

Server: That sounds delicious. What would you like for your two sides?

You: _____

Server: Would you like anything else?

You: _____

Server: I will put in your order.

You: _____

PRACTICE

Part 2 Directions: Write the question for each answer.

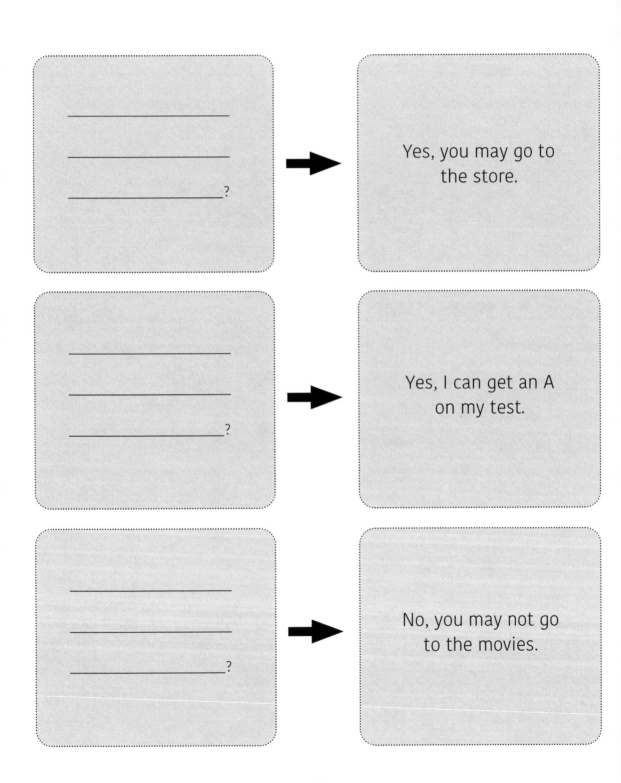

_____ _____ _____? →	Yes, you may go to the store.
_____ _____ _____? →	Yes, I can get an A on my test.
_____ _____ _____? →	No, you may not go to the movies.

PRACTICE

Part 3 Directions: Fill in the boxes of the crossword. Use the clues.

Across
1. round meat in between buns
5. pasta with red sauce

Down
1. long meat in between bread
2. made from potatoes
3. a sweet dessert
4. pie with sauce and cheese

PRACTICE

Part 4 Directions: Think about whether you can, may, or might do the following things. Write can, may or might on the line.

1. Ride a bike _____

2. Do math homework _____

3. Go to college _____

4. Get a dog _____

5. Brush your teeth _____

6. Go to the movies _____

7. Need money _____

8. Go eat at a restaurant _____

9. Count to 100 _____

10. Spell hard words _____

11. Get a cell phone _____

12. Talk to your friends _____

13. Eat cake _____

14. Climb a mountain _____

15. Ask a question in class _____

16. Bake a cake _____

Review and Advancement for Chapters 11 through 15

Chapter 11 Vocabulary Directions: Match the picture to the word. Write the letter in the blank.

_____ 1. baseball   _____ 5. hockey

_____ 2. basketball   _____ 6. stick

_____ 3. football   _____ 7. tackle

_____ 4. skates   _____ 8. touchdown

A.

B.
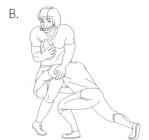

C.

D.

E.

F.

G.

H.

Chapter 12 Vocabulary Directions: Read the story. Then fill in the blank with the correct word from the word box. You will not use all of the words.

> - clothes   • shirt   • socks
>
> - dress   • shoes   • sweater
>
> - pants   • shorts

When I get dressed, I put on my _____. I am a girl, so I might wear a

_____. If it is too cold outside, I will not wear _____ but I will wear

_____ on my legs. I will put on my _____ over my head. Then I will

wear a _____ over that. Last, I put _____ on my feet. Then I put

on my _____.

Chapter 13 Vocabulary Directions: Read the clues for each type of transportation. Write the transportation on the line.

1. _____

tracks

railroad

choo-choo

3. _____

road

school

seats

2. _____

airport

fly

runway

4. _____

parking lot

drive

seat belt

Chapter 14 Vocabulary Directions: Write a sentence about each thing. Write whether you like or dislike it.

1. Do you like to do this?

Listening to music

_____

2. Do you like to do this?

Watching television

_____

3. Do you like to do this?

Playing sports

_____

4. Do you like to do this?

Playing video games

_____

5. Do you like to do this?

Playing outside

_____

Chapter 15 Vocabulary Directions: Fill in the blanks with the correct food.

- cake
- cheese
- hamburger
- pizza
- potatoes
- spaghetti

1. I eat a _____ with lettuce and tomatoes on it.

2. There are noodles and sauce in _____.

3. I ate a slice of _____ on my birthday.

4. Chips are crunchy and made out of _____.

5. _____ is round.

6. _____ is yellow and melts.

GRAMMAR PRACTICE

Part 1 Directions: Fill in the blank with the correct form of the verb that is in parentheses. It should match the subject.

1. The girls _____ basketball. (play)

2. Children _____ in the street. (run)

3. A flower _____ in the garden. (grow)

4. Dogs _____ up and down. (jump)

5. The lamp _____ the hall. (light)

6. A cat _____ on the floor. (crawl)

7. The birds _____ in the trees. (sing)

8. Women _____ flowers. (pick)

9. The children _____ trees. (climb)

10. A player _____ the ball. (dribble)

11. The boys _____ in a car. (ride)

12. Matt _____ to draw. (like)

13. The teacher _____ homework. (give)

14. Students _____ the answer. (write)

15. A person _____ the doorbell. (ring)

GRAMMAR PRACTICE

Part 2 Directions: Match the question starters to each question.

A. How many   B. How much

1. _____ money do you have?

2. _____ coins are in your pocket?

3. _____ time do you have?

4. _____ water is in the glass?

5. _____ dogs are in the house?

6. _____ sweaters do you own?

7. _____ sugar is in the pie?

8. _____ people are in the store?

9. _____ milk is in the bowl?

10._____ ties are on the bed?

11. _____ bugs are on the floor?

12. _____ eyes does a bug have?

GRAMMAR PRACTICE

Part 3 Directions: Unscramble the sentences. Then write them in the correct order.

1. dog house in is the the

_____

2. at boy desk his is the

_____

3. is on table the the vase

_____

4. flowers of out the the took vase we

_____

5. I store the to went

_____

6. door out the we went

_____

7. box in is present the the

_____

GRAMMAR PRACTICE

Part 4 Directions: Draw the picture described. Then write a sentence using "much," "many," or "a lot."

1. Draw a picture of ten flowers.

....

2. Draw a picture of the friendship between two children.

....

3. Draw a picture of five stores.

GRAMMAR PRACTICE

Part 5 Directions: Write a sentence with an action verb and a helping verb.

1. Can + run

_____

2. May + drive

_____

3. Might + cook

_____

4. Can + read

_____

5. May + watch

_____

6. Might + travel

_____

7. Can + study

_____

8. May + play

_____

Test: Chapters 11 through 15

Part 1 Directions: Choose the correct vocabulary word from Chapters 11 – 15 to fill in the blank.

1. You get points in football if you make a _____.

2. Players _____ the ball down the court in basketball.

3. Players hit the puck with a _____ in hockey.

4. You get one point in baseball with a _____.

5. Players throw the ball into a _____ in basketball.

6. Many people _____ to a new city.

7. I wear a shirt and _____ in the summer.

8. The girl wears a pretty _____ to school.

9. People wear different _____ in different weather.

10. Put _____ on your feet first.

11. The airplane landed at the _____.

12. People _____ cars.

13. The _____ is on the tracks.

14. We went to the _____ to see the animals.

15. Children ride the _____ to school.

16. People _____ television.

17. Teenagers like to play _____.

18. Children will _____ their money.

19. People listen to _____.

20. There are two _____ on my bed.

21. You can eat mashed _____.

22. I _____ water.

23. Cakes and cookies are _____.

24. _____ I watch television?

25. Students _____ do their homework.

Part 2 Directions: Read each question. Circle the correct answer from the choices.

1. The football player _____ the ball.
   A. kick   **B**. dribbles   **C**. kicks

2. The football players _____ down the field.
   A. run   **B**. runs   **C**. hit

3. A hockey player _____ the puck.
   A. shoot   **B**. hoop   **C**. shoots

4. The baseball player _____ the ball.
   A. shoot   **B**. hit   **C**. hits

5. A baseball player _____ his bat.
   A. swinging   **B**. swings   **C**. swing

6. _____ money is that shirt?
   A. How much   **B**. How many

7. _____ pieces of cake are left?
   A. How much   **B**. How many

8. _____ cans are there?
   A. How much   **B**. How many

9. _____ chips are in the bag?
   A. How much   **B**. How many

10. _____ food do I need for the trip?
    A. How much   **B**. How many

11. The bed is _____ the bedroom.
    A. in   **B**. at   **C**. on   **D**. out

12. The roof is _____ the house.
    A. to   **B**. on   **C**. at   **D**. in

13. The mailman is _____ the door.

    A. out   **B**. to   **C**. in   **D**. at

14. We walked _____ the door to the front yard.

    A. to   **B**. out   **C**. at   **D**. on

15. The students went _____ school.

    A. at   **B**. in   **C**. to   **D**. out

16. There are _____ of people here.

    A. much   **B**. many   **C**. a lot

17. There is so _____ sadness.

    A. much   **B**. many   **C**. a lot

18. Sarah has _____ sisters.

    A. much   **B**. many   **C**. a lot

19. I know _____ students.

    A. much   **B**. many   **C**. a lot

20. Parents have _____ love for their children.

    A. much   **B**. many   **C**. a lot

21. Billy _____ watch television or listen to music.

    A. can   **B**. may   **C**. might

22. Sarah _____ go to the store if her mother lets her.

    A. can   **B**. may   **C**. might

23. The girl _____ ride a bike. She learned to do that.

    A. can   **B**. may   **C**. might

24. The boys _____ go fishing. Their father said they could.

    A. can   **B**. may   **C**. might

25. I _____ do that. I practiced.

    A. can   **B**. may   **C**. might

Chapter 16: HOLIDAYS AND TRAVEL

KEY VOCABULARY WORDS AND SENTENCES

birthday [bɘrth dā]
Sentence: My birthday is September ninth.

chocolate [chŏk ɘ lĭt]
Sentence: I like to eat chocolate.

Christmas [krĭst mŭs]
Sentence: Christmas is December twenty-fifth.

costume [cŏs toom]
Sentence: We wear costumes on Halloween.

decorations [dĕc ɘr ā shuns]
Sentence: We put up decorations on holidays.

dressing [drĕs ing]
Sentence: I eat turkey and dressing.

Halloween [hăl ō wēn]
Sentence: Halloween is in October.

holiday [hŏl ĭ dāy]
Sentence: I like to celebrate holidays.

lights [līts]
Sentence: I put up lights on the tree.

pinches [pĭnch ĕs]
Sentence: The boy pinches the girl.

presents [prĕz ĭnts]
Sentence: We give presents.

St. Patrick's Day [sānt păt rĭx dāy]
Sentence: St. Patrick's Day is in March.

Thanksgiving [thanks gĭv ing]
Sentence: Thanksgiving is in November.

trip [trĭp]
Sentence: I took a trip.

turkey [tɘrk ē]
Sentence: I eat turkey on Thanksgiving.

vacation [vā cā shun]
Sentence: Take a vacation.

Valentine's Day [văl ĭn tīns dāy]
Sentence: I sent a card on Valentine's Day.

witch [wĭch]
Sentence: I was a witch on Halloween.

wizard [wĭz ɘrd]
Sentence: I was a wizard on Halloween.

wrapped [răp d]
Sentence: We wrapped presents.

GRAMMAR

There are two sets of pronouns. Both sets of pronouns are found together. They are in the same sentence, or in two sentences together.

mine = my/I

yours = your/you

his = him/he

hers = her/she

ours = our/we

theirs = they

EXAMPLES

This is my homework. The homework is mine.

They have two cars. The cars are theirs.

Read the sentences. Look for the pronouns in the sentence. See the possessive pronouns.

1. He has a cat. The cat is his.

2. You have a dog. The dog is yours.

3. My mom has flowers in her garden. The flowers are hers.

4. We own a house. The house is ours.

5. They have a television. The television is theirs.

6. She pulls out her homework. The homework is hers.

PRACTICE

Part 1 Directions: Fill in the blanks of the text conversation. Think about the holiday.

It is the end of October. It is Halloween!

_____

I am getting dressed up, too. I will be a witch.

_____

How are you doing? It has been almost a month since I talked to you!

_____

Yes, we will be having a great dinner, too, with turkey and dressing.

_____

PRACTICE

Part 2 Directions: Read the poems below. Write down the holiday that is described in the poems.

1. _____

> With a heart in my hand
> And a card just for you
> I sent you some flowers
> And chocolates, too!

2. _____

> A tree is put up
> With lights all around
> Presents are wrapped
> And wait to be found.

3. _____

> I'm dressed up in costume
> To get something sweet
> I knock on the door
> And yell, "Trick or Treat!"

4. _____

> Bunches of presents
> And only for me
> We're having a party
> Because I'm now fifteen.

PRACTICE

Part 3 Directions: Fill in the blank with the correct pronoun.

1. I like my book. The book is _____.

2. Tom's table is next to the door. The table is _____.

3. Sarah is carrying her vase. The vase is _____.

4. Our family owns a house. The house is _____.

5. We have a dog. The dog is _____.

6. You have a room. The room is _____.

7. Sam and Steve have a car. The car is _____.

8. Karen has a lamp. The lamp is _____.

9. The pencil is in my hand. The pencil is _____.

10. She has a restaurant. The restaurant is _____.

11. Molly and Tim own a cat. The cat is _____.

12. They have a job. The job is _____.

PRACTICE

Part 4 Directions: Read the story. Then answer the questions in complete sentences.

Sally calls her best friend. Her best friend is Sarah. Sally has not talked to her best friend in a year. They talk about what they did last year.

Sally celebrated New Year's Day by being with friends and family. Sarah celebrated Valentine's Day by sending cards. Sally celebrated Halloween by dressing up in a costume.

On Thanksgiving Day, both girls ate dinner with their families. On Christmas Day, both girls opened presents.

1. Who is Sally's friend?

_____

2. On what holiday do the girls eat dinner with their families?

_____

3. What do both girls do on Christmas Day?

_____

4. What does Sarah do on Valentine's Day?

_____

5. What does Sally do on New Year's Day?

_____

Chapter 17: DESCRIPTION

KEY VOCABULARY WORDS AND SENTENCES

beautiful [bū tĭ ful]
 Sentence: The girl is beautiful.

dead [dĕd]
 Sentence: The man is dead.

field [fēld]
 Sentence: We walked into the field.

firemen [fīr men]
 Sentence: The firemen put out the fire.

fire truck [fīr trŭc]
 Sentence: The fire truck drove up
 to the fire.

good [good]
 Sentence: I am good at math.

great [grāt]
 Sentence: She is great at English.

hoses [hōs ĕs]
 Sentence: The hoses pour out water.

large [lärj]
 Sentence: I have a large family.

long [lŏng]
 Sentence: This is a long test.

loud [lowd]
 Sentence: My dog has a loud bark.

medium [mē dē ŭm]
 Sentence: I wear a medium shirt.

pond [pŏnd]
 Sentence: We fish in the pond.

pretty [prĭt ē]
 Sentence: The girl is pretty.

short [shȯrt]
 Sentence: My friend is short and not
 tall.

small [smŏl]
 Sentence: She is small.

smoke [smōk]
 Sentence: Fire makes smoke.

ugly [ŭg lē]
 Sentence: The dog is ugly.

GRAMMAR

Adjectives describe nouns

They can be:

* sizes—small, medium, large

* colors—blue, green, red

* numbers—two, four, 100

EXAMPLE SENTENCES

Read the sentences. The adjectives are underlined. Think about what noun the adjective describes.

1. We see the red heart.

2. The three boys ran across the street.

3. Everyone heard my loud dog.

4. I wore a large shirt.

5. Sarah loves her four cats.

6. My angry mom yelled at us.

7. The doctor helped the sick man.

8. Kevin has a small ring on his finger.

9. Our neighbor has a big house.

10. The teacher told us to read twelve pages.

PRACTICE

Part 1 Directions: Look at the picture. Unscramble the sentences with the adjectives. Use the picture for help.

1. boy his next short sister stood tall the to

_____

_____

_____

_____

2. a long man the took walk

_____

_____

_____

_____

3. an Christmas sweater the ugly wears the girl

_____

_____

_____

_____

PRACTICE

Part 2 Directions: In each box, write a sentence with an adjective in it. Each sentence must be about the picture.

PRACTICE

Part 3 Directions: Answer the questions about yourself.

DESCRIBING YOURSELF

1. Are you tall or short?

_____

2. Do you have a large or small nose?

_____

3. Do you have long or short hair?

_____

4. Do you have a large or small family?

_____

5. How many clothes do you have?

_____

6. What color is your house?

_____

PRACTICE

Part 4 Directions: Read the story and look at the picture. Then answer the questions.

A fire truck races to a fire. The white house is on fire. The firemen use hoses. Water comes out of the hoses. The boy is scared. A fireman helps the boy and his mother. Some people are in the white house. The firemen try to save them. Everyone is scared. Smoke comes out of the house. Cars drive by on the road.

1. How many firemen are there? _____

2. Is the white house big or small? _____

3. Is the ladder tall or short? _____

4. Is the hose long or short? _____

5. Is the boy tall or short? _____

6. What color is the smoke? _____

7. What color is the fire? _____

8. How many people are in the picture? _____

9. What are the firemen doing? _____

Chapter 18: DAILY ACTIVITIES

KEY VOCABULARY WORDS AND SENTENCES

clean the room [clēn the room]
Sentence: Sarah cleans the room.

do the laundry [do the lŏn drē]
Sentence: We will do the laundry.

dryer [drī er]
Sentence: We put the clothes in the dryer.

eat breakfast [ēt brĕk fĭst]
Sentence: She eats breakfast in the morning.

get dressed [gĭt drĕs d]
Sentence: I get dressed first.

make the bed [māk the bĕd]
Sentence: I make the bed.

skill [skĭl]
Sentence: I have skills.

stretches [strĕch ĭs]
Sentence: He stretches his arms.

wake up [wāk ŭp]
Sentence: We wake up early.

washer [wŏsh ǝr]
Sentence: I put my clothes in the washer.

weekend [wēk end]
Sentence: I like to party on the weekend.

yawns [yŏns]
Sentence: Steve yawns in the morning.

GRAMMAR

PRESENT TENSE VS. PRESENT CONTINUOUS TENSE

PRESENT TENSE: Happening now or every day.

Verbs in the present tense do not have a helping verb.

Examples: runs, walks, rides

PRESENT CONTINUOUS TENSE: Happening now and continues to happen.

Verbs in the present continuous tense do have a helping verb.

Examples: is running, are walking, am riding

Read the sentences below. Look at the verbs.

1. I am running to school.

2. I run to school.

3. They are eating dinner.

4. They eat dinner.

5. We are reading a book.

6. We read a book.

7. She is helping us.

8. She helps us.

9. He is learning the skill.

10. He learns the skill.

PRACTICE

Part 1 Directions: Read about what is happening for each person. Then write a sentence about what they are doing as their daily activities.

1. A girl puts food in her mouth. She has eggs and bacon on her plate. It is early in the morning.

_____

2. A boy opens his eyes. He stretches his arms into the air. He yawns and gets up.

_____

3. A mother picks up the clothes. These are clothes that are dirty. She puts them in the washer and then puts them in the dryer.

_____

4. A woman takes off her night clothes in the morning. Then she puts on work clothes. Then she goes to work.

_____

5. A girl gets up. She takes the sheet and pulls it up. Then she takes the cover and pulls it up. Then she puts the pillows back in place.

_____

6. A boy puts his toys away. He picks up his dirty clothes. He puts them in a basket.

_____

PRACTICE

Part 2 Directions: Look at the picture. Write a sentence about what is happening right now (present tense) and what will go on happening (present continuous tense.)

1. _____

2. _____

3. _____

4. _____

5. _____

PRACTICE

Part 3 Directions: Read the email. Then write a few sentences responding to the email.

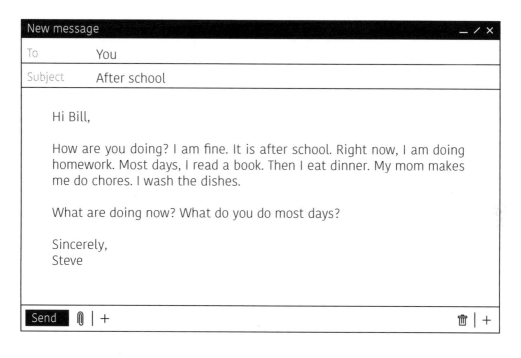

New message   — / ✕

To   You

Subject   After school

Hi Bill,

How are you doing? I am fine. It is after school. Right now, I am doing homework. Most days, I read a book. Then I eat dinner. My mom makes me do chores. I wash the dishes.

What are doing now? What do you do most days?

Sincerely,
Steve

Send   📎 | +   🗑 | +

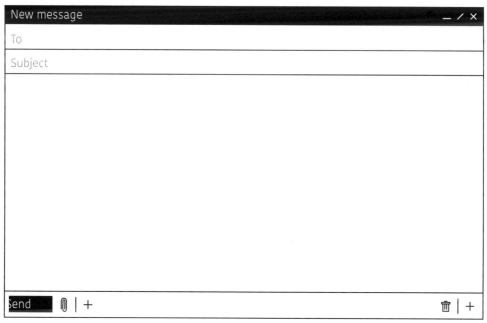

New message   — / ✕

To

Subject

Send   📎 | +   🗑 | +

PRACTICE

Part 4 Directions: Answer these questions about yourself. Write them in complete sentences.

Daily Activities

1. Do you ride in a car every day?

2. What do you do in the morning?

3. When do you brush your teeth?

4. Do you ride a bicycle every day?

5. When do you watch television?

6. Do you eat lunch every day?

7. What do you do after school?

8. Do you like to read books?

9. Do you play sports?

10. What do you do on the weekends?

Chapter 19: MANNERS

KEY VOCABULARY WORDS AND SENTENCES

ate [āt]
Sentence: I ate food.

birthday party [bƏrth dā pär tē]
Sentence: We had a birthday party.

bring [brēng]
Sentence: Bring your book to class.

brought [brŏt]
Sentence: I brought a book to class.

cash [cash]
Sentence: I paid in cash.

eat [ēt]
Sentence: Eat your breakfast.

folder [fōld Ər]
Sentence: I put my paper in my folder.

keep [kēp]
Sentence: Keep the door open.

kept [kĕpt]
Sentence: I kept the door open

paid [pād]
Sentence: I paid for my food.

pay [pā]
Sentence: Please pay for your food.

please [plēs]
Sentence: Say please.

said [sĕd]
Sentence: She said something.

sat [săt]
Sentence: I sat in the chair.

say [sā]
Sentence: Say your name.

secrets [sē crĕts]
Sentence: She keeps secrets.

sit [sĭt]
Sentence: I sit in the chair.

thank you [thänk ū]
Sentence: Say thank you.

think [thēnk]
Sentence: I think of an idea.

thought [thŏt]
Sentence: I thought of an idea.

GRAMMAR

IRREGULAR PRESENT AND PAST TENSE VERBS

sit	sat
think	thought
bring	brought
eat	ate
buy	bought
keep	kept
pay	paid
say	said

Remember: PRESENT TENSE VERBS ARE HAPPENING RIGHT NOW.
PAST TENSE VERBS HAPPENED BEFORE RIGHT NOW.

READ THE SENTENCES BELOW. FIND THE VERB. THINK OF ITS PRESENT TENSE.

1. Sarah sat at the table.

2. We thought of an idea.

3. Karen brought a salad to dinner.

4. I ate a hamburger yesterday.

5. They bought a car.

6. We kept a secret.

7. Sally paid for lunch.

8. "Look!" said Martha.

PRACTICE

Part 1 Directions: Circle the verb. Write whether it is in the present or past tense.

1. My family bought a new car.

      CIRCLE: PRESENT   PAST

2. I thought about the new job.

      CIRCLE: PRESENT   PAST

3. We sit in tall chairs.

      CIRCLE: PRESENT   PAST

4. My aunt brought her baby to the party.

      CIRCLE: PRESENT   PAST

5. The boys eat a large pizza.

      CIRCLE: PRESENT   PAST

6. Sarah kept the children in the room.

      CIRCLE: PRESENT   PAST

7. I paid for the house in cash.

      CIRCLE: PRESENT   PAST

8. We run a race.

      CIRCLE: PRESENT   PAST

PRACTICE

Part 2 Directions: First, read each sentence. Find the verb. Next, rewrite the sentence. If the verb is in the present tense, rewrite the sentence with the past tense of the verb. If the verb is in the past tense, rewrite the sentence with the present tense of the verb.

1. Karen sits at the table.

_____

2. Sam brings the flower to the desk.

_____

3. We bought the right stuff.

_____

4. You pay to eat at a restaurant.

_____

5. The boy keeps his papers in a folder.

_____

PRACTICE

Part 3 Directions: Choose the right word for each blank.

1. Open the door, _____.

      A. please

      B. thank you

      C. sit

2. We _____ in our chairs yesterday.

      A. thought

      B. sat

      C. bought

3. Sarah _____ for my dinner earlier at the restaurant.

      A. bought

      B. said

      C. paid

4. I got your present. _____!

      A. Please

      B. Thank you

      C. No

5. Right now, we _____ lunch.

      A. ate

      B. eat

      C. buy

PRACTICE

Part 4 Directions: Write a verb for each noun. What verb goes with that noun?

1. Chair

_____

2. Idea

_____

3. Gifts

_____

4. Secrets

_____

5. Food

_____

6. Words

_____

Chapter 20: FUTURE EVENTS

KEY VOCABULARY WORDS AND SENTENCES

born [bòrn]
Sentence: I was born in 1977.

college [cŏl ĭj]
Sentence: I went to college.

drive a car [drīv a car]
Sentence: I drive a car to work.

future [foo chur]
Sentence: I will go to college in the future.

get a job [gĭt a job]
Sentence: I will get a job tomorrow.

get married [get mār ēd]
Sentence: I will get married in a few years.

graduate [grăd ū ĭt]
Sentence: I will graduate from school.

have children [have chĭl drĭn]
Sentence: I have two children.

marriage [mār ĕj]
Sentence: My marriage is good.

retire [rē tīr]
Sentence: I will retire from my job.

shall [shăl]
Sentence: I shall go to college.

will [wĭl]
Sentence: I will go to the store tomorrow.

GRAMMAR

FUTURE TENSE VERBS

To make a future tense verb, include:

Will or shall + the verb

Read the sentences. Think about how these events happen in the future.

1. I will walk to school tomorrow.
2. She shall turn in her homework.
3. My mom will go to work tomorrow morning.
4. Our father will like to do that.
5. Everyone shall be happy soon.

PRACTICE

Part 1 Directions: Read the discussion. Fill in the blanks with the correct words.

Friend: What will you do tomorrow when you turn sixteen?

You: _____

Friend: What will you do after high school?

You: _____

Friend: What will you do after you meet someone you really like?

You: _____

Friend: What will you do to make money?

You: _____

Friend: What will you do later in life?

You: _____

Friend: That sounds like a good plan.

You: _____

PRACTICE

Part 2 Directions: Write the question for each answer.

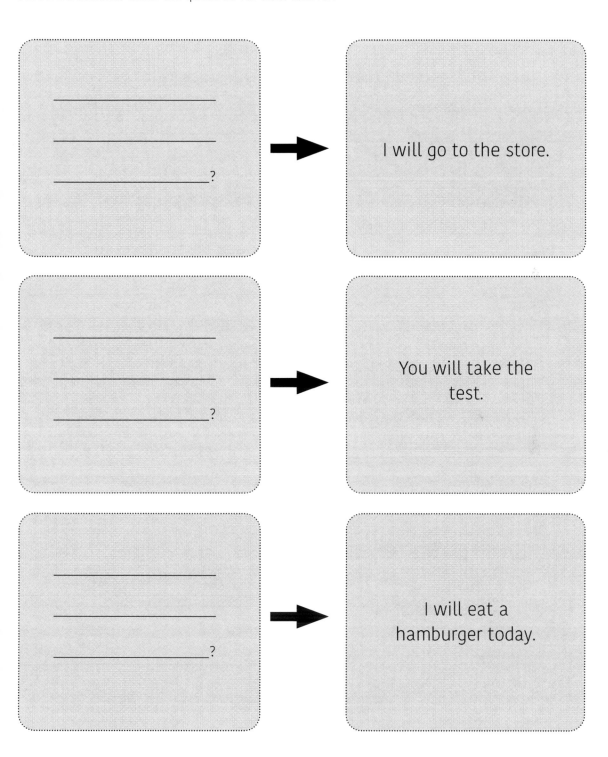

_____

_____

_____ ?   →   I will go to the store.

_____

_____

_____ ?   →   You will take the test.

_____

_____

_____ ?   →   I will eat a hamburger today.

PRACTICE

Part 3 Directions: Use the clues to fill in the boxes of the crossword.

Across
2. something you do to make money
3. something you do to a car
5. get together with someone

Down
1. education after high school
4. what you do after you have worked a long time

PRACTICE

Part 4 Directions: Think about when you would do this activity. Then write a sentence about whether you would do this in the past, present, or future. Use the right verb tense.

1. Do homework_____

2. Be born _____

3. Go to college _____

4. Eat a meal _____

5. Learn to ride a bike _____

6. Walk the dog _____

7. Get married _____

8. Have children _____

9. Retire from work _____

10. Go to school _____

11. Drive a car _____

12. Make friends _____

13. Go to a restaurant _____

14. Take a vacation _____

15. Go to class _____

16. Take a test _____

REVIEW AND TEST OF THE BOOK

Part 1 Directions: Look at the vocabulary words in the box. Look at each picture. Label the picture, or write down, where you find each vocabulary word in the picture.

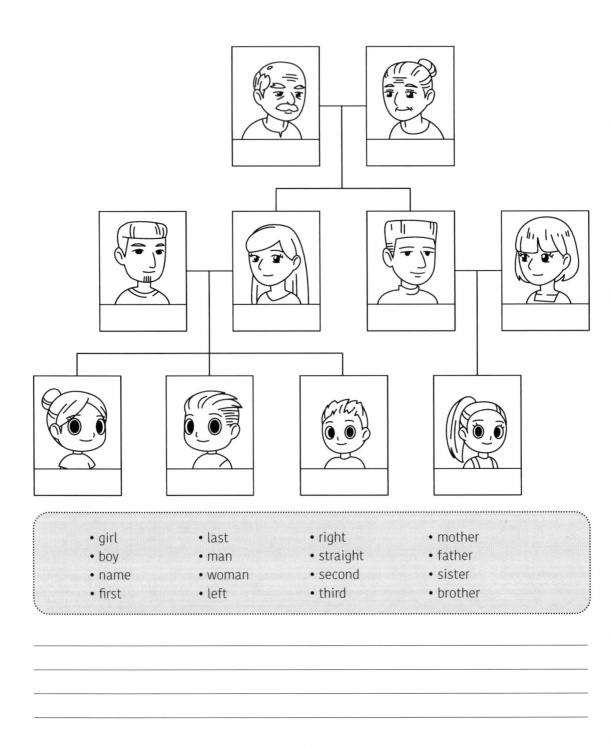

- girl
- boy
- name
- first
- last
- man
- woman
- left
- right
- straight
- second
- third
- mother
- father
- sister
- brother

_____

_____

_____

_____

- living room
- kitchen
- bedroom
- bathroom
- hall

		1	2	3	4	5
6	7	8	9	10	11	12
13	14	15	16	17	18	19
20	21	22	23	24	25	26
27	28	29	30	31		

- Friday
- Monday
- Saturday
- Sunday
- Thursday
- Tuesday
- Wednesday

Part 2 Directions: Draw a person. Then label the parts of the body, or the parts affected by the sickness.

- head
- face
- arms
- legs
- shoulders

- knees
- feet
- hands
- eyes
- nose

- mouth
- ears
- headache
- stomachache
- cold

Part 3 Directions: Write down the vocabulary word for each definition or synonym.

JOBS

1. AT A HOSPITAL: _____
2. AT A SCHOOL: _____
3. AT A BARBER SHOP: _____
4. AT A POLICE STATION: _____

FOOD

5. FRIED POTATOES: _____
6. MEAT ON A BUN: _____
7. CHEESE AND SAUCE ON ROUND DOUGH: _____
8. SWIMS IN THE OCEAN: _____

PAST EVENTS

9. WHAT YOU DO TO A ROOM: _____
10. WHAT YOU DO IF YOU GET A GIFT: _____
11. WHAT YOU DO AT YOUR JOB: _____
12. WHAT YOU DO TO A BALL: _____

SPORTS

13. HOOP, DRIBBLE: _____
14. HOME RUN, BAT: _____
15. STICK, PUCK, SKATES: _____
16. BALL, TOUCHDOWN: _____

CLOTHING

17. A SHIRT WITH A SKIRT TOGETHER: _____
18. TWO THINGS YOU PUT ON YOUR FEET: _____
19. WHAT YOU WEAR IN THE SUMMER: _____

TRANSPORTATION

20. AT AN AIRPORT: _____
21. ON TRACKS: _____
22. ON THE ROAD: _____

HOBBIES:

23. PLAY _____

24. WATCH _____

25. LISTEN TO _____

26. PLAY VIDEO _____

HOLIDAYS

27. WITH PRESENTS: _____

28. HEARTS: _____

29. EATING TURKEY: _____

30. DRESS IN COSTUMES: _____

ADJECTIVES THAT MEAN THE SAME

31. PRETTY: _____

32. NOT PRETTY: _____

33. TINY: _____

34. BIG: _____

DAILY ACTIVITIES

35. EAT _____ IN THE MORNING

36. WAKE _____

37. GET _____ (CLOTHES)

38. MAKE THE _____

FUTURE EVENTS

39. SCHOOL AFTER HIGH SCHOOL: _____

40. LOVE SOMEONE: _____

41. DRIVE A _____

42. STOP WORKING: _____

Part 4 Directions: Choose the correct answer.

1. I _____ your mom.
     A. am   **B**. is   **C**. are

2. The girls _____ nice.
     A. am   **B**. is   **C**. are

3. The boys _____ here.
     A. am   **B**. is   **C**. are

4. _____ is your mother? My mother is Shelly.
     A. Where   **B**. When   **C**. Who

5. _____ is your mother? My mother is over there.
     A. Where   **B**. What   **C**. Which

6. _____ is it time to go? It is time to go at noon.
     A. When   **B**. Who   **C**. Where

7. I like _____friends.
     A. me   **B**. my   **C**. your

8. She has _____ homework.
     A. her   **B**. his   **C**. my

9. The boy knows _____ name.
     A. his   **B**. it   **C**. you

10. What month comes before February?
     A. June   **B**. July   **C**. January

11. What month comes right after March?
     A. May   **B**. April   **C**. September

12. What day comes right before Wednesday?
     A. Monday   **B**. Tuesday   **C**. Thursday

13. _____ apple is on the table.
     A. A   **B**. An

14. _____ girl is next door.

   A. An   **B**. The

15. _____ boy right there is next.

   A. A   **B**. The

16. _____ a flower.

   A. There is   **B**. There are

17. _____ two students.

   A. There is   **B**. There are

18. _____ my sister.

   A. There is   **B**. There are

19. _____ hot dogs are ready.

   A. This   **B**. These

20. _____ lamp is on.

   A. That   **B**. Those

21. We _____ to the store yesterday.

   A. walk   **B**. walked   **C**. will walk

22. Sarah _____ to the store tomorrow.

   A. go   **B**. went   **C**. will go

23. The dog _____ all day long every day.

   A. barks   **B**. barked   **C**. will bark

24. _____ money do you have?

   A. How much · **B**. How many

25. _____ arms do you have?

   A. How much   **B**. How many

FINAL TEST

Directions: Write three sentences for each question, or set of questions, below. Make sure you use adjectives, prepositions, and the correct subjects and verbs in each sentence.

1. Who are the people in your family? What are their first and last names?

_____

_____

_____

2. How do you get from your house to school?

_____

_____

_____

3. Who are you? What is your name and age?

_____

_____

_____

4. What rooms are inside your home? What are the things in these rooms?

_____

_____

_____

5. When is your birthday? What are your favorite holidays and when are these holidays?

_____

_____

_____

6. How do you feel today? How do you feel when you get sick?

_____

_____

_____

7. What job do you want?

_____

_____

_____

8. What foods do you like and dislike? What hobbies do you like and dislike?

_____

_____

_____

9. What did you do yesterday?

_____

_____

_____

10. What is your favorite sport?

_____

_____

_____

11. What clothes are you wearing?

_____

_____

_____

12. What will you do in the future?

_____

_____

_____

CONCLUSION

Congratulations on a job well done! You should now understand how to hold a short conversation in English with somebody else. You are well on your way to becoming better at communicating in English.

If someone asks you, you may be able to give simple directions to help him or her get to their destination. You should be able to write a short note in English to someone, including the vocabulary that you learned. You can go around your house and identify the rooms in it. If someone gets sick, you may be able to tell them what sickness they have and where that sickness is located in their body.

However, you should not stop now. Remember that learning a language like English takes time and is a continuous process. You should consider practicing English at your job, if possible, and in your daily activities.

Since you have now learned the basics of the English language, you can continue your learning by moving on to another level of English. The next step is to take a class in English that is designed to reinforce what you have learned from this book. After that, you can complete another book that will take you to the next level of speaking English.

In addition to book study, be sure to communicate in English with native English speakers. This will help you learn the common expressions, slang, and figurative language that English speakers use in their conversations. So, don't give up! There are many opportunities out there, both online and in many parts of the world, where you can learn to easily and fluently write, read, listen to, and speak English.

ANSWER KEY

Chapter 1

Part 1 Practice:
Answers may vary slightly but may include:
Hi! Who are you? = Hi! I am fine!
My name is Jim. What is your name? = My name is Tina.
I am Sam. Who are you? = I am (student's name).
Kim, how old are you? = I am 5 years old.
Are you a student? = Yes, I am.
How old are you? = I am 10.

Part 2 Practice:
Hi = Hi
My name is Lil. = My name is (student's name).
Are you a student at school? = Yes, I am a student.
Do you go to school? = Yes, I go to school.
How old are you? = I am (student's age).

Chapter 2

Part 1 Practice:
Where is the woman?
Who is the person?
When did the woman go to the drugstore?
What did the woman get at the drugstore?
Which drug did the woman get?

Part 2 Practice:
"First, go straight on Main Street. Next, turn right on Pine Street. Then, turn right on Maple Street. Next, turn right on River Street. Go straight on River Street. Then turn left on Hill Street. Last, turn left on Grove Street. You are now at the school!"

Chapter 3

Part 1 Practice:

Down:
1. Patty to Tim – cousin
2. May to Kim - aunt
3. Bill to Tim, Kim, Sam and Patty - grandfather
5. Amy to Tim and Kim - mother
6. Tim to Kim - brother
7. Ted to Tim and Kim - father

Across:
4. Kim to Tim - sister
8. Sue to Tim, Kim, Sam and Patty - grandmother
9. Ted to Sam – uncle

Part 2 Practice:

Me: Aunt Sarah is at the house.
Me: Great! Grandfather is coming.
Uncle: No, I have not heard from your sister.

Chapter 4

Part 1 Practice:

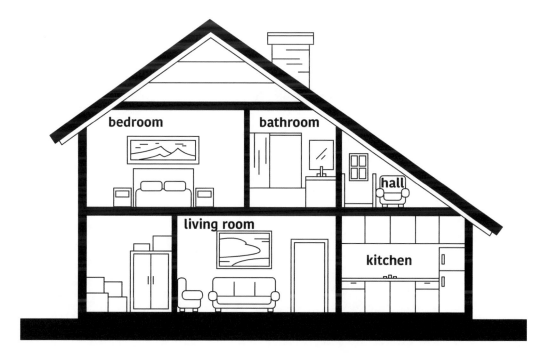

Part 2 Practice:
1. Kitchen
2. Living room
3. Bathroom
4. Hall

Chapter 5

Part 1 Practice:

1. J	11. K
2. E	12. A
3. G	13. G
4. C	14. E
5. I	15. C
6. L	16. A
7. H	17. B
8. D	18. F
9. B	19. D
10. F	

Part 2 Practice:
1. The day is Sunday.
2. The month is May.
3. The day is Tuesday.
4. The month is January.
5. The month is July.

Review and Advancement for Chapters 1-5

Chapter 1:
School, boy, girl, students
Down, road, town
Seven years old, new, old, age

Chapter 2:
turn left, turn right, go straight, first, second, third

Chapter 3:
grandfather, grandmother, mother, sister, father, brother

Chapter 4:
bathroom, bedroom, dining room, kitchen, living room

Chapter 5:

January, February, March, April, June, July, August, September, October, November, December

Match:

1. A	7. C	13. D	19. A
2. C	8. C	14. B	20. D
3. C	9. C	15. C	21. A
4. B	10. A	16. A	22. B
5. B	11. E	17. D	23. A
6. B	12. B	18. B	

Test

1. am	6. What	11. He	16. children
2. are	7. When	12. it	17. January
3. is	8. Who	13. cat	18. February
4. are	9. She	14. cats	19. March
5. Where	10. her	15. child	20. July

Chapter 6

Part 1 Practice:

I feel sick.	I am angry.
I feel well.	I have a stomachache.
I am happy.	I have a headache.
I am sad.	I have a cold.

Part 2 Practice:

2. Across - your
4. Across – their
6. Across – its
1. Down – her
3. Down – our
5. Down – his

Chapter 7

Part 1 Practice:

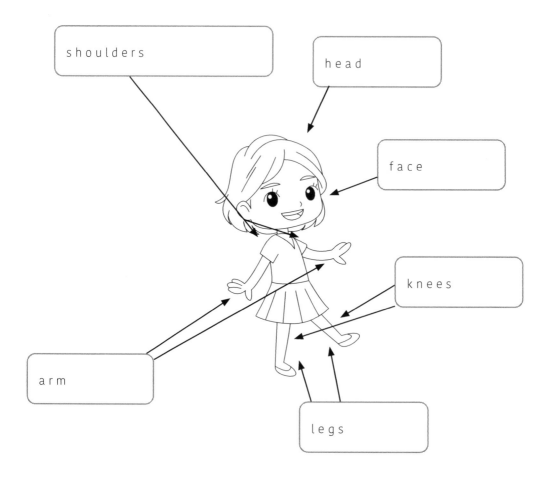

shoulders

head

face

knees

arm

legs

Part 2 Practice:
I need a scarf. It is so cold outside. You have a scarf. May I use the scarf, please? Also, I need an umbrella. It may rain today. May I use the umbrella at your house?

Chapter 8

Part 1 Practice: Answers will vary.

Part 2 Practice:

There is a nice policeman.
There are boats in the water.
There are plants in the ground.

There are five flowers.
There is a star in the sky.
There are five doctors in the hospital.
There are some papers in my notebook.

Chapter 9

Part 1 Practice: Answers will vary, but they must begin with "I like…" or "I dislike…"

Part 2 Practice:
This phone, paper, computer
That clipboard, pencil
These books
Those envelopes, binders

Chapter 10

Part 1 Practice: Answers will vary.

Part 2 Practice: Answers will vary.

Review and Advancement of Chapters 6-10

Chapter 6
1. E
2. F
3. D
4. C
5. H
6. B
7. A
8. G

Chapter 7
Sarah saw a dog down the road. She sees with her eyes. Then she smelled a rose. She smells with her nose. She found a dog. The dog ate food. The dog eats with his mouth. Sarah fell over the dog. She fell onto her knees. Blood dripped down her legs. Then her mother called to her. She heard her mother with her ears. She put her hands on Sarah's wound. It stopped the bleeding.

Chapter 8
1. Dentist
2. Teacher
3. Barber
4. Policeman
5. Nurse or doctor

Chapter 9
Answers will vary, but they will begin with "I like…" or "I hate…"

Chapter 10
1. thanked
2. burned
3. kicked
4. pulled
5. dressed
6. cleaned
7. cooked
8. walked
9. carried

Part 1:
She walked her dog.
The dog dug its hole.
I love my dog.
He ate his pizza.
They talked on their phones.
You like your dress.
The ant carried its food.
I ate my food.
We followed our children.
They ran to their schools.
You want your cake.
I like my book.
He asked his question.
They sat on their steps.
We looked at our shoes.
You did your work.
She did her homework.
The cat licked its paw.
He loves his hair.
She called her friend.
We drove to our house.

Part 2:
1. The
2. A
3. An
4. The
5. the
6. the
7. a
8. the
9. the
10. the
11. a
12. A

Part 3:
1. There are two books on the table.
2. There is a chair.
3. There is a pillow on the bed.
4. There are four children at the park.
5. There is an apple in the bowl.
6. There are dogs in the backyard.
7. There is a cat on the chair.
8. There are three beds in the house.
9. There are many doctors in the hospital.
10. There is an ice cream cone.

Part 4: Answers will vary, but sentence 1 should include "these." Picture 2 should include "that." Picture 3 should include "this." Picture 4 should include "those."

Part 5:
1. thanks, thanked
2. burns, burned
3. cleans, cleaned
4. dresses, dressed
5. walk, walked
6. carries, carried
7. cooks, cooked
8. kick, kicked
9. pulls, pulled

Chapter 6-10 Test

Part 1:
1. paw
2. shot
3. stomachache
4. nurse
5. bone
6. mouth
7. eyes
8. ears
9. feet
10. arms
11. barber
12. teacher
13. hospital
14. policeman
15. dentist
16. books
17. computer
18. phone
19. hotdog
20. hamburger
21. burns
22. cook
23. pull
24. kicks
25. clean

Part 2:

1. D
2. D
3. B
4. B
5. A
6. C
7. C
8. B
9. A
10. A
11. A
12. B
13. B
14. A
15. B
16. A
17. C
18. B
19. D
20. C
21. B
22. D
23. C
24. B
25. A

Chapter 11

1. Subject – dogs; verb – bark = plural
2. Subject – cat; verb – meows = singular
3. Subject – child; verb – yells = singular
4. Subject – sister; verb – tells = singular
5. Subject – mom; verb – walks = singular
6. Subject – students; verb – write = plural
7. Subject – men; verb – read = plural
8. Subject – children; verb – paint = plural
9. Subject – birds; verb – fly = plural
10. Subject – man; verb – drives = singular
11. Subject – teachers; verb – grade = plural
12. Subject – barber; verb – cuts = singular
13. Subject – nurses; verb – give = plural
14. Subject – Karen; verb – eats = singular
15. Subject – door; verb – opens = singular
16. Subject – Molly; verb – talks = singular
17. Subject – Sarah; verb – watches = singular
18. Subject – girl; verb – sits = singular
19. Subject – maid; verb – cleans = singular
20. Subject – she; verb – dresses = singular

Part 1 Practice:
Answers may vary, but should include the correct subject verb agreement.

Part 2 Practice:
1. Basketball
2. Hockey
3. Baseball
4. Football

Part 3 Practice:
Answers may vary, but the most obvious answers are below.

1. see
2. shoot
3. hits
4. runs
5. skates

6. hop
7. sleeps
8. plays
9. gives
10. brush

Part 4 Practice:
1. Tim plays basketball first.
2. Tim likes basketball.
3. Tim skates around the rink and plays hockey.
4. Tim plays baseball at the baseball field.
5. Tim plays basketball first.

Chapter 12

Part 1 Practice:
Answers will vary, but they should be written in the same way as the sentences below.
1. There are 200 candies in the jar.
2. The diamond ring costs $1,000 dollars.
3. There are eight ounces of water in the cup.

Part 2 Practice:
How much does this purple dress cost?
This purple dress costs $25.
How much does the red dress cost?
The red dress costs $17.
How many dresses do you have?
We have 4 dresses.
How many pants do you have?
We have 12 pants.

Part 3 Practice:
Answers will vary, but the sentences should be written in the same format.
1. I have 3 brothers.
2. I love my parents a lot.
3. I own 2 pets.
4. I have no money.
5. I eat one sweet in a day.
6. I study a lot for tests.

Part 4 Practice:
1. The apples cost $5.95.
2. Sam buys 2 apples.
3. The wine costs $8.25.
4. Sam drinks the wine at dinner and sometimes after dinner.
5. The turkey costs $8.95.
6. Sam buys 3 meats.
7. Sam buys cheese because his children like to eat cheese sandwiches.
8. His children drink the milk.
9. The milk costs $1.30.
10. Sam buys 2 fish.
11. The fish costs $7.00.
12. The steak costs $9.95.
13. The meat costs $25.90 altogether.
14. Sam buys 4 apples and bananas total.

Chapter 13

Part 1 Practice:
1. Airplanes
2. Cars
3. Trains

Part 2 Practice:
1. Ball
2. Sandcastle
3. Dog

Part 3 Practice:
Answers will vary, but the response should include how the person is doing and how the person will get there by their choice of transportation.

Part 4 Practice:
Answers will vary, but the sentences should be in the same sentence format. Below are examples of what the answers could be.
1. Yes, I ride in a car to school.
2. I ride a bus in the afternoon.
3. Yes, I have been in an airplane.
4. I go to the airport to fly in an airplane.
5. Yes, I have a train in my city.
6. I fly in an airplane to go to another city.
7. Trains are fast.
8. Airplanes fly in the sky.
9. I have seen 3 airplanes.
10. My family has 2 cars.

Chapter 14

Grammar Activity:
1. Not counted
2. Not counted
3. Not counted
4. Counted
5. Counted
6. Counted
7. Counted
8. Counted
9. Not counted

Part 1 Practice:
Sentences will vary, but an example has been included.
1. Yes; I have many blankets.
2. No; Thank you so much for your friendship.
3. Yes; I have a lot of dogs.
4. Yes; There are a lot of pillows on my bed.
5. No; There is much love between the two people.
6. Yes; I have many books.
7. No; There is a lot of happiness.

Part 2 Practice:
1. Sports
2. Television
3. Listening to music
4. Video games
5. Read

Part 3 Practice:
1. B
2. D
3. C
4. D
5. B
6. A

Part 4 Practice:
Answers will vary.

Chapter 15

Part 1 Practice:
Answers will vary, but these responses are an example.
I would like to drink water.
Yes, I would.
I would like a steak.
I would like green beans and mashed potatoes.
No, I would not.
Thank you.

Part 2 Practice:
May I go to the store?
Can you get an A on the test?
May I go to the movies?

Part 3 Practice:
1. Across – hamburger
5. Across – spaghetti
1. Down – hotdog
2. Down – fries
3. Down – cake
4. Down – pizza

Part 4 Practice:
Some of these answers may vary.

1. Can	9. Can
2. Can	10. Might
3. Might	11. May
4. Might	12. May
5. Can	13. May
6. May	14. Might
7. Might	15. Can
8. May	16. Can

Review and Advancement of Chapters 11-15

Chapter 11

1. E	5. H
2. C	6. F
3. G	7. A
4. D	8. B

Chapter 12
clothes, dress, shorts, pants, shirt, sweater, socks, shoes

Chapter 13
1. Train
2. Airplane
3. Bus
4. Car

Chapter 14
Answers will vary, but the sentence format should be the same as the examples below.
1. I like listening to music.
2. I hate watching television.
3. I like playing sports.
4. I hate playing video games.
5. I like playing outside.
6. I like watching sports.

Chapter 15
1. hamburger
2. spaghetti
3. cake
4. potatoes
5. pizza
6. cheese

Grammar Practice

Part 1
1. play
2. run
3. grows
4. jump
5. lights
6. crawls
7. sing
8. pick
9. climb
10. dribbles
11. ride
12. likes
13. gives
14. write
15. rings

Part 2

1. B	7. B
2. A	8. A
3. B	9. B
4. B	10. A
5. A	11. A
6. A	12. A

Part 3

1. The dog is in the house.
2. A boy is at his desk.
3. The vase is on the table.
4. We took the flowers out of the vase.
5. I went to the store.
6. We went out the door.
7. The present is in the box.

Part 4

Answers will vary, but each sentence should include the following.
1. many or a lot
2. much
3. many or a lot

Part 5

Answers will vary.

Chapters 11-15 Test

Part 1

1. touchdown	14. zoo
2. dribble	15. bus
3. stick	16. watch
4. homerun	17. video games
5. hoop	18. spend
6. move	19. music
7. shorts	20. pillows
8. dress	21. potatoes
9. clothes	22. drink
10. socks	23. sweet
11. airport	24. May
12. drive	25. can
13. train	

Part 2

1. C	14. B
2. A	15. C
3. C	16. C
4. C	17. A
5. B	18. B
6. A	19. B
7. B	20. A
8. B	21. C
9. B	22. B
10. A	23. A
11. A	24. B
12. B	25. A
13. D	

Chapter 16

Part 1 Practice:
Answers may vary, but they may include the following:
Are you going to wear a costume?
I am going to be a witch too.
Yes, it has been a long time. Are you going to have turkey at Thanksgiving?
That sounds delicious.

Part 2 Practice:
1. Valentine's Day
2. Christmas
3. Halloween
4. Birthday

Part 3 Practice:

1. mine	7. theirs
2. his	8. hers
3. hers	9. mine
4. ours	10. hers
5. ours	11. theirs
6. yours	12. theirs

Part 4 Practice:
1. Sarah is Sally's friend.
2. On Thanksgiving, the girls eat dinner with their families.
3. They open presents.
4. Sarah sends cards on Valentine's Day.
5. Sally celebrates New Year's Day with friends and family.

Chapter 17

Part 1 Practice:
1. The tall boy is next to his short sister.
2. The man took a long walk.
3. The woman wears an ugly Christmas sweater.

Part 2 Practice:
Answers will vary, but they may include:
The short mouse jumps.
The big elephant rides a small bike.
The gray elephant looks at the mouse.
The happy mouse looks at me.

Part 3 Practice:
Answers will vary, but they should be written in the same format.
1. I am tall.
2. I have a small nose.
3. I have long hair.
4. I have a large family.
5. I have many clothes.
6. My house is blue.

Part 4 Practice:
1. There are fourteen firemen.
2. The white house is large.
3. The ladder is tall.
4. The hose is long.
5. The boy is short.
6. The smoke is gray.
7. The fire is yellow.
8. There are many people in the picture.
9. The firemen are putting out the fire.

Chapter 18

Part 1 Practice:
1. The girl eats breakfast.
2. The boy wakes up.
3. The mother cleans the clothes.
4. The woman gets dressed.
5. The girl makes the bed.
6. The boy cleans his room.

Part 2 Practice:
Answers will vary.

Part 3 Practice:
Answers will vary, but the response should include how the person is doing, what they are doing now and what they do most days.

Part 4 Practice:
Answers will vary, but they should be written in the sentence format below.

1. I ride in a car every day.
2. I get dressed in the morning.
3. I brush my teeth in the morning.
4. I do not ride a bicycle every day.
5. I watch television after school.
6. I eat lunch every day.
7. I play sports after school.
8. I like to read books.
9. I play sports.
10. I listen to music on the weekends.

Chapter 19

Grammar Activity
1. sat – sits
2. thought – thinks
3. brought – brings
4. ate – eats
5. bought – buys
6. kept – keep
7. paid – pays
8. said – says

Part 1 Practice:
1. bought – past
2. thought – past
3. sit – present
4. brought – past
5. eat – present
6. kept – past
7. paid – past
8. run – present

Part 2 Practice:
1. sits – Karen sat at the table.
2. brings – Sam brought the flowers to the desk.
3. bought – We buy the right stuff.
4. pay – You paid to eat at a restaurant.
5. keeps – The boy kept his papers in a folder.

Part 3 Practice:
1. A
2. B
3. C
4. B
5. A

Part 4 Practice:
Answers will vary, but they may include:
1. Sit
2. Think
3. Give
4. Keep
5. Eat
6. Speak

Chapter 20

Part 1 Practice:
I will get my driver's license.
I will go to college after high school.
I will get married.
I will get a job.
I will retire from my job.
Thank you.

Part 2 Practice:
Where will you go?
What will do you at school?
What will you eat today?

Part 3 Practice:
2. Across – job
3. Across – drive
5. Across – married
1. Down – college
4. Down – retire

Part 4 Practice:
Answers will vary, but they may include if this is a child the following answers.

1. Present – I do my homework today.
2. Past – I was born years ago.
3. Future – I will go to college.
4. Present – I eat a meal right now.
5. Past – I learned to ride a bike.
6. Present – I walk the dog.
7. Future – I will get married.
8. Future – I will have children.
9. Future – I will retire from work.
10. Present – I go to school.
11. Future – I will drive a car.
12. Present – I make friends.
13. Present – I go to a restaurant.
14. Past – I took a vacation.
15. Present – I go to class.
16. Present – I take the test today.

Review and Test of the Book

Answers will vary, but an example is below.

Vanessa is a girl and Justin is the boy. Jessica is a first name. Smith is a last name. Angela is a woman on the right. Alan is a father. He is on the left. Jessica's picture is straight below Joseph. Jessica is the mother. Alan is the father. Vanessa is the sister to Justin. Michael is the brother to Linda.

The living room is next to the kitchen. There is a table in the living room. The bedroom has a bed in it. The father cooks in the kitchen. The bathroom is next to the hall. There is a closet in the bedroom.

The first day is Sunday. The second day is Monday. The third day is Tuesday. The next day is Wednesday. Thursday is after Wednesday. Friday is the last day of school. Saturday is the last day.

A person should be drawn and the correct body parts should be labelled as well as where each sickness would affect.

Vocabulary

1. Nurse or doctor
2. Teacher
3. Barber
4. Policeman
5. Fries
6. Hamburger
7. Pizza
8. Fish
9. Clean
10. Buy
11. Work
12. Kick
13. Basketball
14. Baseball
15. Hockey
16. Football
17. Dress
18. Socks and shoes
19. Shirt and shorts
20. Airplane
21. Train
22. Car or Bus
23. Sports
24. Television
25. Music
26. Games
27. Christmas
28. Valentine's Day
29. Thanksgiving
30. Halloween
31. Beautiful
32. Ugly
33. Small
34. Large
35. Breakfast
36. Up
37. Dressed
38. Bed
39. College
40. Married
41. Car
42. Retire

Multiple Choice

1. A
2. C
3. C
4. C
5. A
6. A
7. B
8. A
9. A
10. C
11. B
12. B
13. B
14. B
15. B
16. A
17. B
18. A
19. B
20. A
21. B
22. C
23. A
24. A
25. B

Test

Answers will vary, but check for complete sentences and that the answers are correct.

Made in the USA
Monee, IL
14 February 2024

53521515R00122